$\mathcal{T}$he
VOICE
of
SUCCESS

$\mathcal{T}$he
VOICE
of
SUCCESS

A Woman's Guide to a
Powerful and Persuasive Voice

Joni Wilson

American Management Association

New York • Atlanta • Brussels • Chicago • Mexico City • San Francisco
Shanghai • Tokyo • Toronto • Washington, D.C.

Special discounts on bulk quantities of AMACOM books are
available to corporations, professional associations, and other
organizations. For details, contact Special Sales Department,
AMACOM, a division of American Management Association,
1601 Broadway, New York, NY 10019.
Tel: 212-903-8316. Fax: 212-903-8083.
E-mail: specialsls@amanet.org
Website: www.amacombooks.org/go/specialsales
To view all AMACOM titles go to: www.amacombooks.org

This publication is designed to provide accurate and authoritative information in
regard to the subject matter covered. It is sold with the understanding that the
publisher is not engaged in rendering legal, accounting, or other professional
service. If legal advice or other expert assistance is required, the services of a
competent professional person should be sought.

Library of Congress Cataloging-in-Publication Data

Wilson, Joni
The voice of success : a woman's guide to a powerful and persuasive voice / Joni Wilson.
    p.   cm.
  Includes bibliographical references and index.
ISBN-10: 0-8144-1280-7
ISBN-13: 978-0-8144-1280-0
1. Voice culture—Exercises.   I. Title.
PN4197.W53   2009
808.5—dc22
                2008052509

Printing number

10   9   8   7   6   5   4   3   2   1

"Never in the history of this planet has there been a more pivotal time to be a woman with a strong, persuasive voice!" *The Voice of Success* is dedicated to that woman.

Contents

Acknowledgments

I would like to personally thank my agent Lilly Gharemani, who first recognized the need of a voice book for women. Throughout the writing process she "kept the faith" and was always there to encourage and inspire me. Thank you to Ellen Coleman for her wisdom, insight, and talented editing and to copyeditor Debbie Posner whose expertise brilliantly pulled it all together. A big thank you to Ellen Kadin, Executive Editor of AMACOM Books, for standing behind *The Voice of Success* and enabling every woman to learn how to create the strong, effective voice she needs to deliver her message. And a huge thanks to all of the women throughout the years who have entrusted me with the most important business asset they possess, their Voices of Success!

The
VOICE
of
SUCCESS

((1))

"Can We Talk?"

An Overview

I was presenting a workshop on Voice Survival at the National Speakers Association Conference in Hollywood, California, when one of the female presenters approached me in the hallway. "Joni, can you help me?" she asked in a raspy voice, "My speech is in two hours and I don't know what to do . . . I have to speak in front of eight hundred professional speakers and my voice is completely gone." She stared at me hopefully, waiting for my answer.

Stop right there and hold that thought while I backtrack eight years to the time when I had just finished writing my first book on voice. Having spent the weekend in an inspiring motivational seminar with Mark Victor Hanson and Jack Canfield, the authors of all those *Chicken Soup for the Soul* books, I was flying high with enthusiasm and untapped potential. I was ready to establish myself as *the* voice expert—not just another voice teacher.

In the years that followed that powerful weekend, I attended many workshops and conferences, sometimes as the presenter/ speaker and sometimes as an attendee. At many of the events, following my presentation on voice techniques, women—speakers and business professionals—often approached me looking for answers to what seemed to be their never-ending voice problems. As my reputation as a voice expert grew, I received telephone calls and e-mails at all hours of the day and night from women searching for answers to those success-robbing voice dilemmas that seemed to pop up at the worst possible times. The problems, which ranged from chronic vocal fatigue to total voice loss, often occurred for no apparent reason. But, of course, there is always a reason.

Over the years, I've worked with female teachers, lawyers, politicians, speakers, singers, business executives, media professionals, and even stay-at-home moms. They were all experiencing voice problems caused by straining their voices as they tried to be heard above life's boisterous noise and chatter.

I understood their frustration because I too had lost my voice at a pivotal time in my life, and that catastrophe almost ended my singing and acting career just as it was about to take off. I was twenty years old, singing in Las Vegas with the world by the tail, when my voice problems began. I had just been booked as an opening act for Elvis (the real one!), and people were actually coming to see *me*. I had wonderful opportunities flying at me from all directions and a secret fear—that I could not trust my voice to be there when I needed it—which kept me from acting on any of them. Like most women with voice problems, I just kept pushing my poor, abused voice by tightening, forcing, and strangling it into submission. In my ignorance, I actually believed that I could make my voice perform by pushing it harder and forcing it to be louder. The frustrating result of all that pushing was, when I pushed it too hard, my voice would wisely say, "Enough is enough, Joni," and completely shut down. It would simply thumb its nose at me and take a mini vacation while I canceled gig after gig and missed opportunity after opportunity because I had no voice.

Like Aristotle searching for the meaning of life, I went from voice teacher to voice teacher searching for the perfect voice method to solve my problems. Nothing was working and I was inconsolably turning down those once-in-a-lifetime possibilities, while watching my career sink like the *Titanic*. My voice had always been the focal point of my work and my true joy in life. Then, to top it all off, a leading throat specialist dispassionately told me, "Forget about singing Joni, your voice is shot. Go find another career." Fortunately, I did not take his advice.

Why You Need a Voice Book Designed Especially for Women

It wasn't until I became a voice teacher eighteen years ago that I realized this problem was not mine alone. I knew there had to be an answer, not only for me, but for all of the women whose livelihoods depended on strong voices that would last for more than a few hours, even when they were overworked and tired.

I spent the next eighteen years watching the answers unfold before me, student by student and lesson by lesson. Each person became a link in a chain of events that, I'm happy to say, completely resolved my voice problems as well as those of my clients. My tenacious search for answers paid off. Today my voice is stronger than ever, which is why I know I can help you find your perfect voice—one that will let you share your message with confidence and control.

Knowing that your voice will be there when you need it most eliminates fear and builds the self-trust so essential for success in every business situation. In my years of teaching, I have seen shy, soft-spoken women perform minor miracles once they learned how to use their voices properly. Sharing this important information is the reason I wrote this book.

Well, that's my story; now let's go back to that NSA Conference in Hollywood. Thankfully, there is a happy and successful ending to that stressful cry for help. My answer to the question, "Joni, can you help me?" was, an emphatic, "yes." I *could* help her. We found a quiet corner where I showed her a simple exercise that freed her constricted vocal cords and calmed her anxiety. The whole process took less than ten minutes and she walked away grinning from ear to ear. Two hours later, she gave her speech and received a standing ovation. This is just one of many success stories to let you know that there is a very bright light at the end of the voice tunnel. As you will discover, the beauty of the techniques you will be learning is that you can *instantly* fix your voice problem with a few simple exercises.

The Vocal Difference Between Men and Women

When you get right down to it, the truth is that a woman's voice, like many other parts of her body, is not as strong as a man's. Because of that difference, in this competitive world, where men and women are running neck and neck for the same jobs, women need to know how to get the most out of their voice without killing it. From office politics to world politics, women are now seeking an equal voice. It is vital, therefore, that women learn how to voice their opinions with authority, assurance, and self-confidence. Despite this, many women still are not comfortable employing these vocal traits.

For a woman to compete effectively at work, she needs a strong yet *pleasing* voice. In this world of e-mail, instant messaging, and texting, the sound of your voice often is the first (and sometimes last) impression you will make, whether you are on the phone, at an interview, or attending a meeting or conference. This is especially true in businesses where relationships begin and end with a telephone call. Since we form many personal connections in a business venue, a pleasing, resonant, and confident voice can be an impressive tool for achieving your success. The fact is, from desk to dating, a woman's voice is responsible for many of her triumphs and—sadly—for many of her business and personal failures.

Whether in a classroom, an office, a courtroom, or on stage, too many women go through their entire lives frustrated and unhappy with the sound of their voices, yet, surprisingly, they neither spend the time nor do the work it takes to improve the sound and quality of those voices. Now is the perfect time to invest in your voice image because never have there been greater opportunities for woman who have new ideas and strong voices with which to express them.

Today's Woman Is Not Yesterday's Wimp

For the first time in three thousand years of recorded history, a woman's words as well as her wisdom are beginning to be heard. To be an effective voice for change, a woman needs a voice that is primed and ready for the task. In other words, she needs to design a voice image that is palatable, powerful, and, above all, pleasing to the ear, if she expects anyone to hear what she has to say.

In their successful careers, many women running major corporations, running for political office or even running their families have been scrutinized and criticized for reacting overemotionally to some event. Their critics often misconstrue feelings—or the expression of them—as a character weakness and use the emotions to belittle these women's abilities. Whether it's nature or nurture can be debated, but it's a fact that most women *are* more emotional than men are. It's a part of who we are, and that is not a bad thing! It's when we try to cover up those emotions that our voices *always*—yes always—give us away despite our best efforts to hide our feelings. You cannot fool your voice no matter what your words say. Your best defense against the detractors is to learn the fine art of voice control no matter how distressed and incensed you may be feeling.

The Female Voice: Myths Versus Cold, Hard Facts

There is a great mystery surrounding the female voice and so much misinformation that it's hard to separate the myths from the facts. For a better understanding of your own voice, let's begin by dispelling some of those myths with the facts.

Myth: Your voice begins and ends in your throat.

Fact: Nothing could be further from the truth. To create a powerful, professional speaking voice that will carry to the back of the room and last for hours, you must learn to use your *entire body* to power your voice (see Chapter 3).

Myth: Your weak voice is caused by age or illness and your voice will weaken as you age.

Fact: Not so. A weak voice is caused mainly by vocal abuse, poor technique, and mistaken beliefs about how the voice works. For a woman to gain control over her voice, it's vital that she understands how the voice operates and how to get the most out of it without damaging her vocal cords. With good vocal technique, a woman's voice can actually improve with age (see Chapter 8).

Myth: Vocal technique is the same for men and women.

Fact: Not true. The female voice is unique, complex, and very different from its male counterpart. Due to the difference in size and strength of the vocal anatomy, most of the vocal problems women face are completely unknown to men (see Chapter 6).

Myth: When women try to speak loudly, they become hoarse and eventually lose their voices completely.

Fact: Although many a successful career has been stopped dead in its tracks by the fear of an uncontrolled vocal blowout at the worst possible time, there is no reason for any woman to go through life in fear of losing her voice. With a bit of understanding and some simple vocal techniques she can take control and learn to trust her voice (see Chapter 3).

Myth: Voice training is only for singers, actors, and those in the news media.

Fact: If you use your voice in your career, whatever it may be, you need to learn how to use it effectively. When you consider that over half of all business relationships begin and often end with a phone call, if you are to thrive and advance in a competitive business atmosphere, you need an effective and personable speaking voice (see Chapter 2).

Myth: All voice problems are caused by colds and vocal strain.

Fact: Voice problems can be caused by both physical *and* mental stress. The body's reaction to verbal and mental abuse can severely damage the vocal cords. Some women tighten, restrict, and swallow the words they don't feel safe expressing, which can set up a mental-emotional-physical chain reaction in the body that can put a chokehold on their voices (see Chapter 7).

These are only a few of the misconceptions and mistaken beliefs surrounding the female voice. Throughout this book, we will explore and disprove many others.

One more thing before we begin building your new voice, I would like you to pause for a few minutes to take the following short voice assessment that I give to all of my female clients before we start working together. The object is to get to know your own voice and the easiest way to do that is to zero in on how you really feel about your voice.

Voice Analysis Assessment for Women

The twenty questions that follow can be answered either yes or no. Read each one and for those that describe your voice, put a Y for yes; for those that don't apply, put an N for no. There are no right or wrong answers and no grades to tally. Your goal is to gain a better understanding of your voice on that deeper level where many of the problems begin. Make a copy of this assessment, grab a pencil, and begin.

—— 1. Does the sound of your voice on your answering machine make you cringe?

—— 2. Are you often out of breath when you talk on the telephone or get excited?

—— 3. Do people have difficulty hearing you; are you constantly asked to repeat yourself?

—— 4. Is your voice tired and raspy at the end of your working day?

—— 5. Do you constantly clear your throat?

—— 6. After a day spent talking, do you feel a lump in your throat area?

—— 7. Do coworkers or family members consistently misconstrue your conversations?

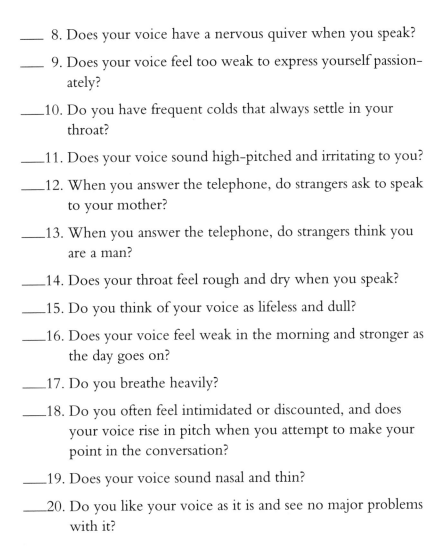

_____ 8. Does your voice have a nervous quiver when you speak?

_____ 9. Does your voice feel too weak to express yourself passionately?

_____10. Do you have frequent colds that always settle in your throat?

_____11. Does your voice sound high-pitched and irritating to you?

_____12. When you answer the telephone, do strangers ask to speak to your mother?

_____13. When you answer the telephone, do strangers think you are a man?

_____14. Does your throat feel rough and dry when you speak?

_____15. Do you think of your voice as lifeless and dull?

_____16. Does your voice feel weak in the morning and stronger as the day goes on?

_____17. Do you breathe heavily?

_____18. Do you often feel intimidated or discounted, and does your voice rise in pitch when you attempt to make your point in the conversation?

_____19. Does your voice sound nasal and thin?

_____20. Do you like your voice as it is and see no major problems with it?

After you have completed your voice analysis, review it to make sure that you have honestly answered the questions. Keep in mind that your only goal is to recognize your own voice problems so we can clear them up and begin designing your perfect voice. If you did not find your particular voice problem listed above, have patience, because in the following pages we will be examining all of the major female voice complaints from TMJ (temporomandibular joint dysfunction—aka "tight jaw") to PMS. We will analyze their effects on your voice, and explore effective ways to control them.

The Gender Voice Thing

The male voice is often preferred over a female voice, especially in business. In training both male and female voices, I learned early on that women are not only at a vocal disadvantage in the workplace because a man has larger vocal cords than a woman does (more on this in Chapters 2 and 8), but, for a variety of reasons both personal and historical, many women fear speaking up (see Chapter 7). This fear spills over into every facet of a woman's private relationships as well as her public image. Even today, many grown women still live in fear of speaking up and "voicing" their needs, likes and dislikes, and emotions; they haven't a clue why their voice remains silent while their brain chatters away. The good news is that just knowing that women have been programmed to keep their mouths shut can be very freeing.

In my workshops, I tell the story of a female friend of mine named Judy who had been an active member of Toastmasters (a wonderful organization of amateur speakers who get together each week to help each another overcome their fear of public speaking). Judy had entered a speech contest, made it to the finals, and was awarded second place. She was noticeably upset when she came in for her next lesson because she believed that she had given the best presentation in the contest and should have taken first place.

When she told me this I asked her the obvious question, "Okay, Judy, if you were the best, as you say you were, why didn't you win?" She looked at me with a bewildered look on her face and said, "I honestly don't know, but I'm mad as hell!"

I had to get to the bottom of this, because I recommend Toast-masters to all of my budding speaker clients, and I had always known their judges to be fair. With a little digging, I found that one of the judges was a former student of mine, so I immediately called her and asked her straight out, "So, what's up with Judy coming in second?"

She agreed that Judy's was the best speech insofar as content was concerned, but the man who won had a beautiful, low, sooth-ing voice. My former student was totally spellbound by the sound of it, as were the other judges—some of whom were men. Men, as well as women, can be charmed by those warm, low, and reso-nant tones.

Two months later, my former student, who had served as the judge, found herself in exactly the same situation. She was a finalist in a speech competition and she, too, placed second. She could hardly wait to call and tell me that she, too, had lost to the same man with the low, resonant voice and minimal content. In both cases, the big prize went to the best voice, *not* the best speech in terms of content or clever presentation.

I don't like to think that I, too, could be influenced by the sound of a voice, but I have to admit that there are times when I would rather sit in a class being soothed by a mellow-toned male voice than have my ears bombarded by an excited, high-pitched female voice. It is just one more of those cold, hard, facts: men have longer vocal cords and bigger bodies than women do, and, since size in large measure determines pitch, men definitely do have the edge.

That doesn't mean that women cannot compete against their male counterparts vocally; it's just that knowing how the game is played, and how to enhance the natural attributes of the female voice image gives women another reason to spend the time, the effort, and the money it takes to create a competitive, yet pleasing, speaking voice. The benefits—professional and personal—could be astronomical and with the right information and guidance, every woman can have a professional-sounding voice that wins applause and earns promotions!

18 Million Cracks in the Stained-Glass Ceiling

Women cannot compete by trying to think and speak like men; their voices cannot and will not take the pressure. Remember, it is not always power and volume that women need in their voices, and even though women are playing hard and well in the gender playground, men will always have the loudest voices.

A perfect example of that power was the 2008 presidential primaries, where a woman (Hillary Clinton) and a man (Barack Obama) battled for votes generated by campaign speeches, debates, and their ability literally to talk the voters into voting for one and rejecting the other. Most in the media agreed that both candidates offered similar solutions and that the woman had more experience than the man did, but many complained about how annoying Hillary's voice was. She was accused of "sounding like my mother nagging at me to clean my room!" by one major CNN talk show host, and of "sounding like my wife asking me to take out the garbage!" by another radio talk show personality. Words like *shrill, screeching, nagging, annoying* were among the many that followed Hillary around the country.

Regardless of politics and choices, just like my friend Judy's speech competition, in this political contest they argued about content, experience, performance, and charisma but during the whole ordeal, I never heard one person in the media complain about Barack Obama's voice.

How important is the sound of a woman's voice in today's world of business and politics? In some cases, that voice can make or break her career. To be successful, a woman needs all of her skills working at full power and that clearly includes her voice.

Have you ever wondered why, when a woman is losing her voice to laryngitis, and has that deep and throaty sound like Kathleen Turner, men find it pleasing, attractive, and very sexy? "Love that voice!" they tell you when you can barely croak out your words. Well, believe it or not, there actually is a physiological reason for that reaction. Just as certain parts of the male/female vocal anatomy are different, the vibrations of a man's hearing mechanism are not the same as a woman's. A high-pitched female voice may simply annoy women, but for the man that she dates, those she works with, and those in her audience, it may actually be *physically painful* to their ears.

For this reason, men do not happily tolerate high-pitched female voices. They automatically block them out no matter how important the information may be or how important the messenger may be; it's nothing personal, it's just a physical, gender reality. You may think a man is blocking out your ideas, but it could very well be your voice that he cannot accept. If you needed another good reason to spend some time improving your voice, that fact alone should do it.

Similarly, how many times have you sat in a meeting or seminar listening to a woman with impressive credentials and a voice that could shatter cement? No matter how earthshaking the information may have been, you just couldn't get past the sound of her voice. Every person in that room was probably asking themselves the same question: "Why doesn't she do something about her voice? Doesn't she know how irritating it is?"

Well, here's another big eye-opener: that speaker does not hear the sound of her voice the way you hear it because inside her head she has large resonating chambers that amplify and fatten her voice. Those chambers give her a false impression that her voice is full and pleasing to the ears of her audience.

- *Fact: Inside your head, you are hearing 65 percent more acoustic sound than is actually coming out of your mouth. What you hear is* not *what your audience hears. The voice in your head is not real!*

The woman speaking does not have a clue that people are cringing as she speaks and missing the importance of the information she is presenting. How sad for her, not to mention the audience that paid good money to hear her speak! Could that woman possibly be you? If so, would your friends be honest and tell you that your voice is annoying their ears? Probably not, just as you will not approach that teacher and tell her how good the class was except for her annoying voice.

As career women, we spend thousands of dollars making sure our outer image is perfect and professional. Not only do we spend years learning our craft and gathering our credentials, we pay through the nose for photos, brochures, websites, business cards, expensive shoes, the perfect outfit, and even plastic surgery, but completely ignore one of the most important assets for our success—our voices.

I Hate My Voice!

Think of the times you have recorded your own voice, especially your voicemail, and been appalled by the sound that comes back at you. I have lost count of how many times, I've heard the words "I hate the sound of my voice! It sounds like I'm five years old" or "I sound so nasal" or "Listen to that accent; I never knew I had one" from my female clients as we play back the audio of their voices. Whether singing or speaking, their reaction is totally predictable: "Does my voice really sound like that?" Their second question, also predictable: "Is there anything I can do to change, strengthen and improve it? With a voice like that, no one is ever going to take me seriously." They are right!

- *Fact: Every day, in both your business and personal life, you are being judged by the sound of your voice.*

It doesn't always have to be that way. With a little bit of understanding, some well-planned practice, and a few simple vocal skills, you could quickly learn to use your voice effectively. A powerful and persuasive voice is a worthy goal for every woman, no matter what her status, age, ethnic background or education may be. No woman needs to be "stuck" with a weak and ineffective voice. A woman's magazine asked me to write an article entitled "Why Women Have Problems Speaking Up." As I began to put my thoughts to paper, it occurred to me that even though I had been training women to speak up and sing out for years, I too have had major problems "voicing" my own truth. Like many of my female friends and students, I had learned to keep my mouth shut to avoid conflicts both at home and in the workplace. Stuffing my voice deep inside for so many years caused major damage to both my singing and speaking voice, as well as to my career and self-esteem.

As I worked on the article, I realized how important it is for women to give themselves permission to speak up and let their voices be heard. Too many women keep silent way too long and then, out of frustration, let their voices erupt in a shrill shriek that shocks the ears so badly no one can hear what is being said, especially the voice-sensitive males within earshot.

R-E-S-P-E-C-T
Your Voice

At some point in their careers, most female singers, speakers, actors, lawyers, teachers, and business professionals unfortunately experience some form of voice problem. If you watch the singers on *American Idol* week after week, you will hear them apologizing for their weak, raspy, voices, and you will also notice that more female contestants complain about this than male contestants. Their problems are not the result of age or illness, because they are all healthy young singers; it is because of overuse, poor voice technique, and/or stress, which can kill a voice faster than anything else can.

Every woman should learn how to control her awesome, but mysterious, female voice. It is vital—no, it is mandatory—that you take the time to learn how your voice works and how to use it to your best advantage. Women must learn to love and respect their own voices if they expect others to listen to them and actually hear their words.

Write this down, tack it on your refrigerator door, and repeat it every day: "If I don't like the sound of my own voice, how can I expect anyone else to listen to it?" How others perceive you is more often than not a reflection of how you perceive yourself.

"I Am Woman Hear Me Roar"—
But Not Today!

The biggest day of your entire career is tomorrow and you have finally been given the opportunity of a lifetime—a chance to show what you've got to the president of your company—and you are *so* ready!

It has taken a month of tedious preparation, from gathering all of your data and putting it in perfect order, to highlighting all of the indisputable facts. Not to mention the graphics in your PowerPoint presentation that look like fine art hanging on the wall of the Smithsonian.

There it is, sitting on the table in front of you, radiating accomplishment from every page of the accompanying report. To top it off, you have even managed to lose those ten extra pounds, which means that designer suit hanging in the closet all winter with the tags still on it is a go!

As you peacefully fall asleep with visions of bonuses dancing in your head, you can't believe how easily everything has come together. Then you open your eyes on the morning of the biggest day of your life to be greeted with a dry scratchy throat and no voice. Your brain screams loudly, "Please, oh please, not my voice, not today of all days. This can't be happening!" but nothing comes out of your mouth but a hoarse whisper. What happened to the voice that was so strong and working flawlessly last night when you were rehearsing your presentation? You, like many before you, have just stepped into a woman's worst voice-loss nightmare. It may sound like an exaggeration but it happens more often then you may think. I know because I am the one they call at 6 A.M. crying, completely convinced that their careers are over, all because of an unpredictable, unreliable female voice.

Many women who depend on a strong voice in the courtroom, classroom, boardroom, or lecture hall, have, to some degree, experienced this frightening, frustrating catastrophe. All of a sudden, a weak, hoarse voice bursts into a perfectly planned day, seemingly from out of nowhere. Is it a cold or a virus? Maybe it was the open window you sat next to at the party last Saturday night. Or, maybe you caught some kind of bug from the guy who sneezed all over you yesterday in the elevator.

You can speculate and "what if" all you want right up until

the very moment of your presentation and still not find a logical answer to the questions "why me, why my voice, why today?" So here comes another female executive beginning *her* important presentation with that same old, tired disclaimer: "I'd like to thank you all for coming today, but before I begin my presentation, I have to apologize for my voice . . . etc., etc., etc."

Too many career women will go through their lives feeling unhappy and insecure about their voices yet do nothing about it. Instead, with a shrug of their shoulders, they try to convince themselves, "That's my voice and I'm stuck with it," which is simply not true.

Your voice is an instrument and to use it correctly you must learn a few vocal skills. Vocal skills are just that—*skills*. You would never consider playing the piano in public without taking lessons and learning good piano technique. The same should be true for your voice. For it to be effective and reliable, even in the worst situations, you must learn to play it correctly.

Freeing Your Voice

Here are seven important truths that will help you free your voice. Read them carefully and make them part of your information base.

1. The voice has no brain of its own. It only believes what you believe. Change your belief about your voice and your voice will change accordingly.

2. A big chunk of your emotional stress accumulates in the jaw causing TMJ and other tight jaw problems. Often a tight jaw is the cause of a tight, constricted voice. A relaxed jaw is vital for strong voice projection that will let you be heard in the back of the room.

3. Whether you are speaking or singing, you and you alone are the master of your vocal instrument. Take the time to learn how to play it correctly and your voice will be a delight to all who hear it, including you.

4. No matter what the size of your mouth may be, for your words to be heard in the back of the room, it must be open.

5. With good vocal technique, your voice will not age. That in itself is worth repeating. Say it one more time, "My voice will not age."

6. Many business colleagues never meet face to face. They know each other only by the sound of their voices. A warm, friendly telephone voice is worth the time it takes to fashion it.

7. If anyone tells you, "Resting your voice will solve all of your vocal problems," don't believe them. Most vocal problems come from overuse and abuse of the vocal cords due to incorrect vocal technique. You can rest them all day, but if you do not learn how to use them correctly, the problems will simply return.

Here are two more bonus "truths" to consider:

1. The human body has not one, but two diaphragms to power the voice—one to compress the air and one to pump it.

2. Vocal nodules (calluses) on the vocal cords (folds) are caused by one thing only—poor voice technique. Surgery won't fix poor technique.

Your Journey Inside Your Voice

As you begin this fascinating journey, keep in mind that your goal is to come to a place where you are the master of your own voice in all situations, both business and personal. The information in this book will give you everything you need to achieve that goal. It's written for today's woman and addresses the challenges she faces daily in her stress-filled, competitive world while pinpointing the negative effects those stresses are causing in her voice. It is filled with simple exercises and solutions to the voice problems only women face. It also comes in an easy-to-understand, conversational (not clinical or technical) language that not only explains why your voice problems occur, but also gently guides you through simple techniques to correct them.

In every woman's fast-paced day, she seldom has time to relax, let alone time to practice voice technique. For this reason, each chapter is filled with exercises you can do in your car on the way to work or at home while taking a shower or preparing dinner. The chapters are designed to stand on their own and can be read in any sequence.

Knowledge is power, and a clear understanding of how your vocal instrument functions is a powerful tool for building the perfect voice with which to deliver your message to the eager ears of a waiting world.

PART I

Effective Communication

How to Use Your Voice to Get What You Want

((2))

Designing a Voice
That Means Business

How to Create a Positive Vocal Image

As more and more women achieve executive, decision-making positions, it's vital to their careers that they learn how to speak with a pleasing yet commanding voice. Actually, today's career woman needs not just one voice for business, but a colorful palette of voices to fit clients, peers, staff, as well as all the diverse situations she encounters daily. In the competitive business world, one voice size no longer fits all.

A woman needs an excellent telephone voice because many of her business relationships still begin and end with a telephone call. She needs a strong, persuasive speaking voice to deliver effective presentations to her clients, and a trained voice for interviews, talk shows, and PR opportunities. She also needs a voice with endurance for classrooms, courtrooms, workshops, and seminars, including teleseminars and webinars. In other words, a woman needs a voice that is versatile and believable.

Tune Up Your Voice Image to Attract Clients

Before we begin creating the perfect voice to deliver your message, take some time to consider carefully how you want it to sound. Most of the women I work with want stronger, lower-pitched voices that command attention and can compete with the voices of their male coworkers. Remember, there are two major differences between the sound of a man's voice and a woman's voice:

1. The size of their vocal cords.
2. The size and strength of the parts of the body that support the vocal cords.

Because of these physical differences, a woman's voice lacks the depth and strength of a man's voice (although there are some women with longer vocal cords and lower voices than the average woman, they are unique and rare). Women in positions of authority, who try lowering their voices to sound more masculine, will often damage the voice and bring about the opposite result, a voice that is weak and raspy. So, how do you create a lower, warmer, and more authoritative voice without damaging your vocal cords? Definitely not by dumping weight on them and trying to make them stretch to sound lower, or by speaking from the back of your throat. Instead, you must learn to use your entire body, including your body's built-in resonating system, to power your voice.

For example, using the high resonator (bridge of the nose), the middle resonator (mouth), and the low resonator (under the chin) effectively will add vocal variety while embellishing and fattening your vocal sound. Having a good understanding of how to use the vowel and consonant sounds also does wonders for your voice dynamics. In addition, you need to master the art of pitch control so the voice does not ascend into the stratosphere when you are excited or descend into the abyss when you are depressed. Most important, you need to learn how to control and regulate your breathing because your voice begins and ends on a breath. Without breath, there is no voice.

Going back to your ideal voice and what it will sound like, ask yourself a few simple questions. Would you like to imitate a female voice you admire or someone you idolized as a child—perhaps your mother or your favorite actress? Many women request a low, resonant voice like Kathleen Turner. I am often asked which female voices I think are ideal for business. My first choice is Diane Sawyer who, I believe, has the perfect feminine, but authoritative voice. It has depth when she wants to create an intimate feeling with her guests, and it can raise just enough to show excitement while remaining pleasant to both the male and the female ear. Keep in mind, as you begin to work on your own voice, that most excellent voices do not just happen—they have taken years to develop.

Voices That Sell, Voices That Don't

When we talk about creating an effective female business voice, what we are seeking is an effective business voice *image*. Because not all business situations are the same, the characteristics of a good female business voice must be able to change with the circumstances. As they say, different strokes for different folks, and in business that means different voices for different business situations. An effective businsswoman must also be an accomplished voice actor playing many parts, and using not just one, but a variety of voices.

To begin the fun—and this will be fun—here is a list of vocal characteristics to browse through and try on for size.

Thirty-Seven Desirable Female Voice Characteristics

Examine the list of vocal characteristics available to you, and then let's begin.

1. Authoritative	14. Intelligent	27. Reserved
2. Beautiful	15. Low	28. Rich
3. Believable	16. Mature	29. Soft
4. Bell-like	17. Melodious	30. Sultry
5. Breath	18. Open	31. Sexy
6. Bright	19. Pleasing	32. Sharp
7. Bubbly	20. Persuasive	33. Silken
8. Clear	21. Polite	34. Smooth
9. Confident	22. Perky	35. Sophisticated
10. Effervescent	23. Powerful	36. Throaty
11. Feminine	24. Relaxed	37. Warm
12. Friendly	25. Round	
13. Intimidating	26. Resonant	

First, I'll describe a business situation and then you pick a voice or voices that go with the territory. For example, assume you are a divorce lawyer representing a woman in a bitter custody battle. Which of the thirty-seven voice characteristics go with that position and situation? I would choose: persuasive, clear, confident, intelligent, mature, powerful, and, of course, intimidating.

I would not hire you if your voice were bubbly, sexy, warm, and friendly. A sales rep should be warm and friendly, not my divorce lawyer. Got the picture?

Let's do another one. If you were in telephone sales, what

voice or voices would you choose? How about warm, confident, persuasive, mature, and friendly?

I would not choose a voice that was too relaxed or too powerful. Too much power over the telephone makes people nervous, especially when it is a female voice.

Now, try this one. If you were giving the welcoming address at the monthly sales meeting, you could choose clear, intelligent, authoritative, and confident. Your voice choice would depend on the type of business your company does. If you were working for a cosmetic company catering to older women, your selection would be quite different from the voice you would choose if you were speaking to a high-tech Internet company full of young aggressive males. When you are speaking to women, you need to be warm, friendly, and very detailed. For the young men, a no-nonsense, get-to-the-point voice would be much more effective. In other words, the fewer words you use to make your point, the more they pay attention. Use too many words and you will lose them.

Most important, however, a business voice must sound natural and believable. A phony-sounding voice is not tolerated in business, especially a phony-sounding female voice. There is nothing more insulting to a client than an insincere voice trying to sound sincere. Note: I am not picking on the female voice. Both male and female voices need to be sincere; that is just good business. However, because of the lower pitch and natural tone of the male voice, a male voice tends to sound more sincere than the higher pitched tone of the female voice. You need to become aware of the differences.

If you were the CEO of an international corporation, what voice characteristics would you need? Definitely authoritative because you would be dealing with people from foreign countries and some cultures still do not recognize women in powerful positions. Your voice would also have to be clear, confident, polite, powerful, and intelligent. If, on the other hand, you were representing an organization dealing with the cultural aspects of a foreign country, you would want to be warm, friendly, authoritative, open—and still intelligent.

A woman in sales, competing with men on an even playing field, would need to be clear, confident, sharp, persuasive, intelligent, and relaxed, but never uptight. A voice image should be flexible and changeable according to the business situation and the intent of the vocal exchange.

Voice Awareness Exercise

Copy the list of voice characteristics and keep it in your daily planner. Observe the people you do business with every day. Study their individual voice characteristics. Ask yourself if any of their voices annoy or irritate you? Which ones are pleasing to your ears? Do their voice characteristics change when they are confronting specific business situations? Now put yourself into the mix. Consider your coworkers and their reactions to you in all types of business situations, the good, the bad, and the ugly.

Awareness is an important ingredient in voice improvement. We are often completely unaware of why people are offended by us or unreceptive to us. We always think it's them and not us. Sometimes it *is* them—but sometimes the problem is us. Curiously, the voice is one aspect of a business image that most people are not aware of.

For example, I have a friend who is very blunt, and I often ask him, "Why do you sound so angry?" He glares at me and angrily replies, "I'm not angry." Yet to me, he appears to be angry. It makes him angry to have to defend himself. This is a voice problem that crosses gender and is rooted in intolerance and impatience with other people. It manifests itself in an angry tone of voice—but my friend has no clue that he sounds angry. While his friends may forgive him, his coworkers try to avoid having conversations with him and his clients seldom return his calls. He often feels left out of the office conversations, and although he is the one with the problem, he is convinced it's "them."

Vocal awareness should be essential for both sexes, but in today's world, it is absolutely mandatory for a woman in both her business and personal relationships. For this reason, we begin honing your vocal awareness by asking you to tune in to the voices around you and take note of how others relate to you when you speak. Watch their body language, their facial expressions, and listen to their tone of voice in your conversations with them.

Your Telephone Voice

The telephone, especially the cell phone, is your lifeline to your world—professional and personal. Over the phone, we fight, profess our love, close huge business deals, lose large sums of money, receive good news, and too often receive bad news. We discuss and decide on some of the most important events in our lives over the telephone. Our conversations can often be emotional, extremely stressful, and very challenging to our voices.

Is it any wonder that all of this talking—especially if it is emotional or stressful—can lead to a very tired voice at the end of a long working day? There was a time when we could leave our telephones at home and escape the constant barrage of words coming at us. There was also a time when we could give our voices a rest, listen to music, and relax while driving to and from work—but no more. Now, our work goes wherever we go, and no excuse is acceptable for not answering an emergency phone call or avoiding an emotional confrontation at work. (See Chapter

7 to better understand how certain emotions affect your voice and how to handle the problems they cause.)

How to Make an Impact on the Phone

To create the perfect business telephone voice, it's important to keep in mind that for most of us, the telephone is predominantly an audio device, and even with text messages and video cameras, hearing is still the dominant sense used when we communicate over the phone. You can do business with people over the phone for years and never know what they look like.

The man in accounting with that low, masculine voice may instantly bring to mind an image of Matthew McConaughey, but he may actually look more like Mr. Whipple squeezing the Charmin. The nice woman in shipping whose gentle helpful voice reminds you of your favorite aunt may actually be an ogre in person, but you formed an instant rapport with her and that has helped immensely when shipping problems come up. Your only link to her is as a faceless voice on the other end of the telephone.

Thus, the opinions you form of the person you are doing business with are based on one thing only—that person's voice.

It is vital, therefore, that you project the correct voice image. The point is this: The sound of your voice over the phone instantly creates an image of who and what you are in the mind of the person on the other end, and that image can greatly influence how well or poorly you interact with this person.

- *The telephone only transmits the voice; it does not enhance it.*

How important is a good telephone voice? If you are a sales person, it can make or break your income; if you are a candidate for a job and trying to get your foot in the door, it can be the difference between getting that interview or not. That's how important it is. (On a personal level, many a woman has fallen madly in love with a voice on the other end of the phone.)

Bottom line: Your voice is your most effective business tool, especially during the first few minutes of a cold call. Let's face it, if clients are turned off by your voice, it's hard to keep them on the telephone long enough to get their attention or their order.

Your Telephone Personality(ies): How Voices Affect Us

Voices not only affect you emotionally, but they can also influence your life as well. The right voice can persuade you to buy a house, switch your phone service, use a certain product, call a lawyer to sue when that product doesn't work, and, if the person is a very good talker, even persuade you to give them your money to invest. (This is especially true if the person's voice reminds you of someone you trust like Uncle Dave or Aunt Sally.)

There is a mystical sense of the unknown surrounding the telephone. When someone cannot see you and knows nothing about who or what you are, you can step outside of yourself and become whoever you choose to be. The person on the other end of the telephone will never know the difference, and this is when your voice-acting ability comes into play.

You can play whatever role it takes to make the client or person on the other end of the line feel comfortable and safe. Developing your own voice personalities to use to brighten up your vocal canvas is a skill every woman in business needs to develop. It is not deceptive, it is just good business.

They Had You from "Hello"

We all have a natural telephone voice personality; that is how we recognize each other by a simple hello. It can be either an asset or a detriment to your business image. I have a girlfriend whose natural telephone voice is very breathy and sexy. It's interesting because when you talk to her in person, her voice doesn't sound that way at all. Some connection between her and the telephone instantly turns her into Marilyn Monroe. Can you imagine the image she creates? It wouldn't work for me, but it seems to work well for her. (She is the receptionist at a men's spa.)

I have a client whose natural voice personality is short and very businesslike. She becomes a butter-would-melt-in-your mouth, warm personality when the telephone rings. I also know a man whose natural voice personality is very stern. Yet he uses a gentle, fatherly voice on the phone, especially when he speaks to women. Whether we are aware of it or not, we are already blessed with multiple personalities—and voices—when it comes to the telephone.

How to Create a Telephone Voice That Sells Your Message

Now let's look at some of the major problems you may encounter in your everyday telephone interactions. To begin, let's take a reality check of your telephone voice personality. I need to emphasize the word *telephone,* because just like my friends, many people completely change their voices when their hands reach for the receiver. How we hear ourselves is seldom how others hear us. By the time the voice has traveled out of your mouth and floats back to your ears, it can become distorted by the traveling space. Even recording your voice is not an accurate sample of your actual sound, especially on a small recording device.

Here are some simple exercises to help you hear what everyone else hears when they call you on the telephone.

Record Your Voice Exercises

Settle down in a nice, quiet place where you will not be disturbed for at least thirty minutes, and please turn off your cell phone. Pick up your favorite book, a magazine, or the local newspaper and begin reading any page aloud into your recorder, speaking just as your favorite female news anchor would. When you have recorded at least fifteen minutes of material, listen to your voice as if it were someone else's. Keep in mind that even the best performers are very critical of their own voices.

Exercise 1: Write down what you like and what you don't like about the voice you hear. Be as honest and objective as possible. Then, using the list of vocal characteristics given earlier in this chapter, analyze your voice. Is it too soft, monotone, too fast or slow and drawn out, too harsh, or high-pitched? Is it emotionless and boring, too muffled (no articulation), or too nasal?

This exercise will help you get to know your voice better so you can pinpoint those areas that need improvement.

Exercise 2: Next, let's see how you sound on your answering machine or voicemail system. Everyone who calls you will hear this voice. Choose a voice from your list and record a new message using that voice; then play it back and, again, be the analyst not the critic. Put yourself in the ears of the person on the other end of your telephone and be honest about what you hear. Does the voice you hear sound warm and friendly, detached and cold, intelligent and trusting, mature, sympathetic, impatient or angry, or—last but not least—sexy?

Ask yourself, "If I heard this voice over the phone, would I want to do business with her?" I hope your answer is yes. If not, try again.

Warming Up the Cold Calls

Now that you have an idea of what you sound like on the other end of the telephone, here is a list of things to do to help you improve your business telephone voice.

1. Take a moment before you make a call to analyze the reason for the call and the reaction you would like the person on the other end to have. Go over the list of voice characteristics and choose those qualities you want to send. Always keep your own motivation in mind.

2. Say your name right up front or the person on the other end may miss your first two sentences trying to figure out who you are. This is a good business practice even if you think they'll recognize your voice. You may catch them at a busy moment when you're not on their mind.

3. Put a smile on your face before you pick up the telephone. If your voice is cold and unfriendly, a smile will not only make you feel better, but it will instantly lighten the sound of your voice. If this sounds strange to you, go back to your recorder and record your voice, first with a frown, then with a smile. The difference is amazing. Save your frown voice for calling someone who owes you money.

4. If you are leaving a message, say your phone number slowly, pausing between the numbers, at the beginning of your message. Repeat it again at the end. If the person misses it once, she or he will have another shot at it. It's annoying to have to repeat an entire message to get a

phone number. Speak directly into the mouthpiece if you have a soft voice. The telephone receiver has a built-in microphone but because some of the lower tones are filtered out in the amplification, a woman's voice can often sound higher and more "childlike" than it really is. This is especially true of inexpensive telephones. If you do business over the phone, invest in a good one.

5. Take a few pant-breaths (see Chapter 6 for details) if you find your voice becoming tense and choked in the middle of an emotional conversation. Tension in the voice is easy to identify. When you feel that lump coming up in your throat, politely say, "Excuse me a moment." Cover the receiver and do a yawn-sigh—Haaaaaaaaa. Then take a few pant-breaths, and come back to the conversation with a relaxed, controlled voice.

The Phone Is Not My Friend: Phone Phobia

The telephone creates panic in the hearts of some, while others spend half of the day with their ear happily glued to it. People who have a natural aversion to the telephone often sound tense and abrupt when using it. If they find themselves in a job that demands a good telephone personality, it can be very stressful. As we have seen, the telephone can affect people in such a way that it alters their entire personality. An otherwise gentle, friendly woman can sound cold and blunt to the person on the other end of the conversation without even be aware of it.

I am one of those people who dreads using the telephone, a holdover from my mother's reaction to bill collectors' calls when I was a child. I have a tendency to avoid calling people back, and I have even been known to hang up when they answer, especially when I don't expect them to answer. The last time I did that, the person on the other end had caller ID and immediately called back asking, "Why did you hang up on me?" Feeling like an idiot, I mumbled something about my telephone not working right. Ever since that embarrassing incident, I have not hung the phone up on anyone. Caller ID cured me of a very rude habit, but I still battle the instant flash of fear of the dreaded unknown, every time the telephone rings.

The tension this fear brings on can be heard in the voice and is easy to identify because it causes the words to sound guarded and strained. If this applies to you, the next time the telephone rings, take a moment before you answer it to pant-breath and relax the vocal cords. A good old yawn-sigh will also do wonders. That one has helped me to keep my own telephone phobia in check.

Telephone Posture

If you do most of your work over the phone while sitting at a desk posture is very important. This is especially true if your work involves reading text over the phone and your eyes are looking down at the text. This causes the entire weight of your head to come down on your larynx. This position puts tremendous weight on the vocal cords, which in turn forces them to work twice as hard to get the job done. By the end of the day, the overworked vocal cords shut down to protect themselves. If you continue to force them to perform under this handicap, you will be left with a raspy, breathy voice at the end of the day. The solution is to buy yourself an inexpensive bookstand to put your papers on so your head can assume a relaxed, upright position, and always sit up straight.

Voice Profiling: America's Dirty Little Secret

From boardroom to podium (lectern) to classroom to telephone, you are judged, labeled, and categorized by the sound of your voice. It is called "voice profiling" (or "linguistic profiling")— and we are all guilty of it. In an instant, you can hear a voice and make a snap decision that this is or is not a person you choose to do business with, perhaps because of the assumptions you make about that person's age, gender, nationality, intelligence, personality, and even emotional stability.

Everyone is aware of racial and age discrimination but most people do not realize that they, too, are being assessed by the sound of their voice—especially on the telephone, where the imagination can run wild. When applying for a loan, scheduling a job interview, renting an apartment, or even arranging a first date, your voice is the big tell-all. What your words say and what your voice is saying are often two different things.

My friend Linda, a staffing coordinator for a law office support staffing service, admits:

> While screening potential candidates I engage in voice profiling on a daily basis. Not by way of prejudice but as part of my job to find the most qualified person for the job . . . [we do] a telephone interview before we bring them in for a face to face. In the first thirty seconds of the telephone interview, I can determine whether I would consider this person for, say, a reception position with a high-profile law firm. Is her voice to tentative? Too soft? Is the pitch easy on my ears? Is there receptivity or reluctance in the voice? Is there optimism or negativity in the voice? Am I able to "hear" her smile? How's the grammar? Does the candidate sound educated and savvy? Is she self-assured or insecure? Is she knowledgeable?

The truth is, a professional interviewer like Linda is trained to tell in thirty seconds—by the voice alone—if a person is qualified for a given job.

Voice profiling in business is a fact of life. The only way to guarantee that you will not be negatively profiled is to make sure that your voice is as professional as your résumé and your hard-earned degrees. A good business voice begins with a good business attitude.

The Six "B" (Business) Attitudes of Voice

Copy or write down the following six attitude adjustments for your voice, and place them next to your business phone:

1. *Be aware.* Know your own voice patterns and personality well.

2. *Be confident.* Believing in yourself will give your voice a confident sound.

3. *Be considerate.* Consideration is becoming a lost art, but don't we love it when it comes our way?

4. *Be a skilled speaker.* Speaking skills are essential in business.

5. *Be persistent.* Perseverance is a virtue in business. "No" does not always mean no.

6. *Be happy.* No one likes to hang out with a stressed-out downer. Happy is not only a state of being; it's an attitude that will show up in your voice. That smile on your face as you pick up the phone will soothe the savage breast on the other end who is ready to take you to task for not sending the merchandise on time. It is very hard to be mad at someone who does not throw mad back at you. Pay attention: This final "Be" will take you all the way to the top.

How to Handle Accents and Dialects in the Workplace

I love working with clients who want to minimize or change their natural speaking patterns. Most of the women come to me asking to minimize a heavy accent that's jeopardizing their career advancement. Because of the accent, those working for them have problems understanding instructions and sometimes have to guess at their meaning—occasionally with disastrous results. From executives in major companies to actors and singers who need to "Americanize" their voices, the frustrations that come from trying to change their cultural heritage are the same.

However, there is often an unconscious underlying reluctance to and resentment about making the necessary changes in their speech patterns. And I've found that most people with accents like the way they speak. They learned how to talk from their parents and they have been speaking that way all of their lives. Whether the accent is regional, class, or ethnic, to change what feels (and sounds) natural to someone, and ask them to sound like someone else could even separate a person from the rest of their family. That underlying feeling of resentment is a huge barrier and blocks the ears of even those who truly believe they want to make this change.

People who come to this country especially for business purposes are often asked by their bosses to Americanize their accent. This request helps them avoid "voice profiling" by clients and coworkers especially if they are in a managerial position. They didn't learn their English from their parents; they learned it in school (here or abroad) or in the course of their work and other social interactions once they got here. Consequently, their emotional attachment is not to their current way of speaking English.

It takes a good understanding of what an accent is and is *not* to give oneself permission to change what is often believed unchangeable.

All the World *Is* Our Stage

Some actresses—Meryl Streep and Gwyneth Paltrow, for example—have that uncanny ability to master accents. Others, like Nicole Kidman (who has a very heavy Australian accent when she is speaking naturally), are able to lose the accent when *playing* an American woman. How do they do that? The same way I help my clients to Americanize their speaking voice without losing their natural accent. The actor simply creates a character that speaks in a voice that fits the part they are playing. It is the same for the businesswoman (or man), who learns to create a character, separate from their natural self, that speaks with an *Americanized* accent. It becomes a game, and not only is the resentment gone, but the fear of losing their "real" identity doesn't even come into play. We are all actors at heart and when we have permission to let that actor out, it is amazing what we can do.

You can read all the books in the library on how to reduce your accent and they will do you no good unless you can actually hear and imitate what you are trying to change. To achieve your goal, you will need to adjust the way you move and use your lips, tongue, teeth and the muscles of your face and jaw. One of the hardest parts of learning new speech patterns is the fact that all of this muscle training changes the way your face looks when you speak. But don't worry, working those facial muscles may look and feel strange, but it gets the job done and exercising stiff facial muscles is never a bad thing for your face.

"Mirror, Mirror on the Wall"

After all is said and done, it comes down to knowing how your natural voice works and having the courage to create effective new ways to use it. Forget the words *accent reduction* and all of the resistance those two words carry with them. Think of this challenge as learning a completely new language in a new voice personality. Erase your concept of how you talk, and approach your new language with the ears of a child, listening and imitating what you are hearing. You are simply adding another voice to your repertoire.

- *This is only your business voice. You can put it in the drawer when you visit the family and take it back out when you are training your staff, or doing business over the telephone.*

Accent-Reducing Exercises

To begin creating this *new you* business voice, first listen to the voices around you and decide how you would like your voice to sound. There are many American accents, depending on what part of the country the speaker comes from—the South, Midwest, East Coast, and West Coast. Each region has its own unique twang and splat. Because Americans are constantly on the move, regional American accents are now mixed into all parts of the country. Listen and find a voice you like, then study not only the sound of the voice but the speaker's facial movements as well.

Next, take out your round standing mirror, set it on a table in front of you, and do the following exercises. Practice moving your facial muscles while watching yourself in the mirror.

Exercise 1: Smile and relax. Do this ten times watching your face in the mirror.

Exercise 2: Put your lips in a pouty kiss position and move them forward and back ten times.

Exercise 3: With your mouth open, move your lips up, down, and sideways.

Exercise 4: With your mouth open, place the tip of your tongue behind your top teeth and say LA, LA, LA, LA (rhymes with ahhhh), dropping the tongue to the bottom teeth on the ahhhh sound. This isolates and strengthens the tip of your tongue.

Again, place your tongue behind your top teeth and say DA, DA, DA, DA, hitting the tongue against the upper gum line like a hammer pounding nails. Again drop it down to the bottom teeth on the ahhhh.

Do these two tongue exercises twenty times each, and, yes, your tongue will get tired and rebel. In the beginning, most women have a hard time opening their mouths wide enough to get that tongue on the top gum line; your job is to stretch and strengthen it.

Exercise 5: While watching your face in the mirror, do your best imitation of your chosen Americanized accent. Read passages with dialogue aloud from your favorite novels or children's book with a variety of characters. Make sure no one is close enough to hear you practice so you don't hold back. Laugh at your faces and giggle at your effort, but keep at it. Remember the fifth "B" attitude of voice is; "Be persistent."

I cover in detail the use of lips tongue, teeth, vowels and consonants in Chapter 4. In addition, there are many good CDs on accents if you become stuck. The point to remember is that you are creating a *new* voice, not changing your old voice.

Bonus: The Fine Art of Listening

For women in business, being a good listener is as important as being a good talker. Learning to turn off that teacher/preacher modus operandi and actually listen to another's ideas and problems is definitely a skill—an important skill that I was missing. I had been a teacher/mother for so many years that my brain clicked into an automatic, "Let me teach you something" gear whenever someone asked a question. This works fine if you are standing in front of a class of people who have paid good money to hear you go on and on; it does not work in a social or business group of peers who have come together to share ideas. There is nothing more annoying or time wasting then one person assuming the role of teacher and forcing everyone else in the group into a listen-only position. To find out if that person could be you, it's time to answer a few short questions to see if you are a good listener, or, like me, you might need some help.

The "Are You a Good Listener?" Test

Answer the following questions yes or no:

1. Do you allow others to finish their thought before jumping in?

2. Are you busy thinking of your story instead of listening to the story being told?

3. Do you dominate the conversation, leaving no open space for others to give their opinions?

4. Do you feel impatient and annoyed if another's story goes past your attention span?

5. Do you manipulate the subject to inject your opinion, disregarding anyone else's participation?

6. Do people look at their watches or politely excuse themselves while you are talking?

7. Do you try to *teach* your opinion or *share* it?

8. Are you bored by other people's opinions?

Whether you are an office manager, the CEO of a major corporation, owner of your own business or a teacher, to be a good communicator requires not only a pleasant sounding voice, but good listening skills as well. A good listener must be *all* of the following:

- Open to new ideas.

- Genuinely interested in the opinions of others.

- Aware of not only what is being said but how it is being said.

- Considerate of the emotional temperature of the speaker.

- Tuned into your own body language (for example, no crossed arms).

- Willing to relinquish the conversation to another while setting aside your own ego, allowing that speaker to shine.

And the single most important skill a good listener needs is:

- Having respect for another's opinions even if those opinions are opposite from your own.

Always remember, a good listener does not argue for the sake of arguing.

Being a good listener will build your clients' and your employees' trust because we all want our voices to be heard.

Becoming a Good Listener

Here are eight tips to help you become a better listener.

1. As the listener, knowing your own body language is as important as knowing your client's body language. Leaning forward into the conversation is a warm, caring gesture; leaning back in your chair with your arms folded is a cold, uninviting gesture.

2. Taking notes during the conversation shows the client or employee that their problem is worth a second look. In their eyes, it also validates the fact that you are listening and have heard what they are saying.

3. Eye contact is very important, both yours and theirs. Don't avoid your listeners' eyes or they will not trust your words.

4. Let the other person talk and tell her or his whole story before you give your opinion. If all of the facts are not on the table, later when they are mentally replaying the conversation, they will not feel confident that you have the complete picture.

5. If you are the owner or manager of the company, hold weekly "listening" meetings and allow your employees to voice their opinions openly. That meeting will help stop any underlying gossip from disgruntled employees.

6. A good listener will repeat what is being said to clarify that she or he has heard it and to verify what is being said. That will stop all of the "she didn't hear a word I said," gripes.

7. Ask questions to get the whole story. Leave nothing to the imagination. Listening takes patience, especially for a busy, no-nonsense executive.

8. Last, but definitely not least, stay focused on your client's problem, not on where you're going to go for lunch when the meeting is over.

These listening tips not only work for your business, but also can be adapted and work magic in your family and with friends. It's well worth the effort.

((3))

"Speak Up! We Can't Hear You in the Back"

How to Become a Vocal Powerhouse

As a ten-year member of the National Speakers Association, I've sat in on literally hundreds of workshops and breakout sessions led by both men and women speakers, authors, business executives, and even comedians. Over the years, invariably when the speaker is a woman, a predictable and annoying male voice bellows from the back of the room, "Speak up! We can't hear you in the back." Even turning up the microphone to feedback level does not solve the problem for him.

The more the speaker tried to up the volume, the thinner, higher, and less audible her voice became. The need to satisfy the disruptor at the back of the room ruined the flow of the presentation and dug a big hole in her self-confidence. If she had known how to use her body to power her voice instead of using that twenty percent in the vocal cord area, she could have satisfied her distracter, taken the focus off her voice, and brought the audience back to the information she was presenting.

Increasing the volume only makes a woman's voice sound thin and strident. So, what is a woman to do when she's having difficulty being heard? The answer lies in her own body.

How to Be Heard Above the Babble

When describing the kinds of voices that are easy to understand and can be heard above the crowd, we use words like *clear, full,* and *strong.* Often, after attending an amazing performance we will say, "She was awesome! Her voice was so rich and *full,* I could hear her all the way in the back of the theater. I'd give anything for a voice like that!" Hold on. Before you give away your first-born, remind yourself that it is not a loud voice that you are admiring—loud is often an assault on our ears—it is that full, rich sound in a voice that takes our breath away.

There is a big difference between *loud* and *full.* Loud tugs on the vocal cords and can do major damage to your voice; full uses that eighty percent body action to keep your vocal cords happy, healthy and working overtime.

A Voice Gone Missing

One of biggest mysteries surrounding the female voice is the *vanishing recording voice syndrome.* Somewhere between recording your message and playing it back, half of your voice seems to disappear. "That's not my voice!" I hear repeatedly from frustrated women who swear that I pressed the wrong button when I played back their recording.

To clear up the mystery, the fact is that what you hear in your head is approximately sixty-five percent louder than what actually comes out of your mouth. There is a logical explanation for this, and it is a vital piece of information that will help you create your optimal voice. The answer is crystal clear: *the voice in your head is not real.*

Your head is filled with open spaces and cavities that make up a natural resonating system. There are three big cavities: the nasopharynx, or sinus cavity, which is your high voice resonator; your mouth, your midrange resonator; and the area between your chin and your larynx, your low voice resonator. The voice in your head vibrates through these open spaces, enhancing your voice like the acoustics in your shower. It's as simple as that.

Your challenge is to create a voice that sounds as full when it comes out of your mouth as it does in your head. Figure 3.1 will introduce you to your natural voice resonating system. Study it well!

The Search for Your Natural Voice

Everyone has a natural voice and it's important to know where yours is, because it's in a place where your vocal pitch is free of any strain or pull and sits in a comfort zone just made for you. Even when your voice is tired and overworked, speaking in your natural voice acts on your vocal cords like a soothing massage. The problem is, when you first hear it, you may swear you sound like Minnie Mouse, but remember: the voice you hear in your head is not what others hear.

Find Your Voice Exercise

How do you find this comfy, soothing spot? It's very simple. If you can close your lips and say "umm-hummm," you can find that sweet spot in your voice. Try it. With lips closed say umm-hummm, making the hummm sound like a siren by pulling the sound of your

Figure 3.1   The Human Resonating System

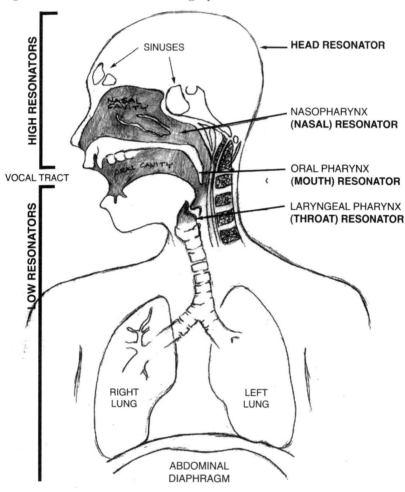

THE HUMAN RESONATING SYSTEM

voice up into your nose (nasocavity). If you tweak your nose like a bunny rabbit—remember Elizabeth Montgomery in *Bewitched?*— on the hummm, it will help pull that sound up into your nose. Watch your favorite pop singer hit those high notes and you will see what a tweaked nose looks like.

Once you have found your natural voice on the umm-hummm, open your mouth and say, "Hello, how are you?" in the exact pitch; do not lower your voice. Now do it again: on the umm-hummm say, "Hello, my name is _____."

Practice this exercise with longer sentences, making sure that you are in your natural voice by putting the umm-hummm in front of all of your words. Inside your head, your voice will sound higher than it used to, but I can assure you no one will even notice the difference. Your voice, on the other hand, will love you for it. (Many voice teachers use this method, but Dr. Morton Cooper, a pioneer in the study of speech and author of the book *Change Your Voice, Change Your Life,* deserves the credit for creating this simple technique.)

How to Achieve Vocal Prowess with the 3-Dimensional Voice® Training System

Throughout my career, I had been searching for that key ingredient that would change my voice from ordinary to extraordinary, from common to uncommon, a component that would add power, strength, and prowess not only to my voice—which I always considered quite average—but also to the voice of every woman looking for a commanding speaking or singing voice.

At the height of my search, my father developed Parkinson's disease and completely lost his voice. Because I was a voice teacher I felt especially helpless as I tried every method I could find to help him find his voice. His mind was sharp as a tack, his eyes were still full of mischief, but his quick wit and sense of humor were silenced because his voice could no longer respond. The doctors said he'd never talk again.

After months of frustrating trial and error, I had exhausted every voice method I knew, but I'm an optimist with a stubborn streak.

I decided to teach him how to use his entire body to add strength to his breath and power his voice. We began by adding depth, the first dimension of vocal sound to his voice; then width, the second dimension for fullness; and last, using his breath, we added length, the third dimension of the voice. To that mix we added the abdominal diaphragm to pump the breath for added length and the pelvic diaphragm to compress the voice for additional power and depth (see Chapters 6 and 7 to learn how to do this). Together, we created the first "3-Dimensional Voice," and wonder of wonders, it worked! Though his speech was slurred, his voice returned, matching that twinkle in his eyes and his sense of humor.

Since then, I have taught the 3-Dimensional Voice Training System to hundreds of men and women who have used it effectively to advance their careers and improve their vocal self-confidence, giving them a voice they could trust and depend on.

What Is a 3-Dimensional Voice and Where Can I Get One?

Most of us associate 3-D with wearing silly glasses and having objects fly at us from a big screen. This is true in the visual world, but not true when it applies to sound. In the world of sound, we can actually hear the effects of using all three dimensions of our voice—depth, width, and length—at once. When a voice moves in all three directions at the same time, it is not only stronger and fuller, it is also easy to access and a delight to the ears. Furthermore, it keeps the strain off the vocal cords by using the entire body to power the voice (for more about this mechanism, see Chapter 6).

The dynamics of the 3-Dimensional Voice training system are based on the movement of sound. Your body is your voice's natural speaker system. When your voice is initiated by the vocal cords, it is only a squeak. As that squeak is projected through the resonating chambers, it will expand, picking up additional resonance and volume as it moves along your vocal track. It's the same principle as sound traveling through a speaker system and it does not take a techno-geek to understand this.

To get the maximum results from all three dimensions of your voice, you must learn how to effectively use every inch of available space in your resonating chambers. Of course the bigger the chambers, the bigger the sound that comes out of your acoustic hole (mouth)—think of Barbra Streisand's nose and Whitney Houston's mouth.

When your voice has a nasal twang to it, it is primarily resonating through your nose or sinus cavity (nasopharynx). When your voice sounds dark, low, feels heavy and tires easily, it is resonating predominately in the lower throat area, located between your chin and your larynx (laryngeal pharynx). If your voice sounds muffled and it's hard for others to understand or hear you, it's because your mouth (oral pharynx), the largest resonating area, is not open wide enough for your words to come forth and be heard (something like shoving a rag in the hole of an acoustic guitar and wondering why it has no sound). Ruling out TMJ, women who do not open their mouths often lack confidence in their message or do not trust their voices to be there when they need it.

To use all three dimensions of your voice correctly takes strong air support and big acoustic spaces. Together they move and amplify your words out of your mouth and into the ears of your listener. Picture those words as lottery balls spinning on a strong column of air (in vocal lingo, it's called "support"). (See

Chapter 6 for an illustration of this.) If you turn *down* the airflow, the lottery balls will lose support and stop spinning. If you turn *off* the airflow, the balls will all fall down—and so will your voice. A weak flow of air creates a weak voice. To completely run out of air causes the voice to dissipate along with the airflow. If you want to keep your voice strong and steady, your must keep a vigorous stream of air pumping up through your vocal cords and out of your mouth.

- *Remember, controlling your air keeps you in control of your voice.*

The best way to utilize your acoustic resonating system is to learn to play it like an instrument, which means using your higher—but not screaming high—tones to create excitement, and your lower tones to add warmth and sincerity to your words. This adds much needed vocal variety to your message. Of course, it takes practice and skill to do this, but the result is well worth it.

When all three of your vocal dimensions—depth, width, and length—are working together in balanced harmony, the result is a beautiful, power-filled voice that will not only serve you well even in times of stress, but also will last your entire lifetime. Your new voice will also make you smile every time you hear it played back in a video, on a CD, or over your voicemail. Now isn't that worth a little work on your part?

"Please Excuse My Voice Tonight"

When I faced a failing career because my voice had become weak and unstable, traditional voice training didn't resolve my problems. To sing today's music and to survive in the competitive business marketplace, I needed more range, more power, more endurance, and more control. Most of all, I needed to enjoy my singing and speaking career, and not live in fear every time my feet hit the stage or podium. I had a love/hate relationship with my career because of my voice. I loved to sing, speak, and share information with my audience, but I hated the stress, pressure, and self-doubt that came with it. When I learned how to master my breathing, and move my voice in three directions at once, producing the power and fullness I had been missing, speaking at conferences, singing with my band for four hours a night, and teaching voice six hours a day became a delight, not a burden. The best part was I no longer had to apologize for my voice, or lack of it. The more I used those three dimensions to power my voice, the stronger it got.

I have been teaching this simple 3-Dimensional Voice technique for over twelve years now. It started with my father and has evolved over the years with each student who successfully applied it. I have fine-tuned it now to the point where, given the right information, instant results can and do happen. (This is the technique I used with the speaker at the NSA conference.)

The Dreaded Vocal "Blowout"

One of the most frustrating turn-of-events a woman can experience is a complete vocal "blowout" right before her big day. Because this chapter is all about adding volume and power to your voice without killing it, it is important to touch on this career halting subject.

It is called a vocal blowout because when the voice is pushed too far in the wrong direction, it finally stops working. Fortunately, you can avoid this state of affairs by keeping your voice in that dropped larynx position and at the same time using the three dimensions of your body for power and strength.

Avoiding Blowouts

Here are five simple steps you can take to help you avoid vocal "blowout."

Step 1: Warm Up Your Voice

A good voice warm-up is as essential to a speaker/singer as it is to a world-class athlete. You would never think of jumping into any physical activity that uses your body without first warming up your muscles. Your vocal mechanism is also composed of muscles that need to be stretched and warmed. This is not only true for your vocal cords; it is also true for your entire body, which is *also* part of your vocal instrument. Your vocal warm-up begins by first relaxing your head, neck, and shoulder area, then doing basic neck and shoulder rolls as follows.

- Roll your head first to the right ten times, then to the left ten times.

- Drop your head to your chest then back as far as it will go ten times.

- Lift and drop your shoulders ten times.

- Do ten shoulder rolls to the front and then ten back.

Do these four exercises very slowly with your eyes closed. A relaxed upper torso is vital to a good vocal warm-up. When you have finished, proceed to the following warm-ups:

- Put your right hand three inches below your sternum (breastbone) at your abdominal diaphragm, open your mouth and pump the air in, filling the bottom of your lungs with air, and without stopping, slowly pump the air out, moving it from your lungs, up through your vocal cords (depth) and out your mouth (length). Feel your diaphragm pumping air in and pushing it back out of your wide-open mouth.

- Now add a big long Haaaaaaaa (yawn-sigh) as the air goes out. Do this twenty times starting on a higher note each time like a siren. Simply slide down the scale from the starting note until you reach the lowest note in your vocal range. Then move up to a higher note with each yawn-sigh until you reach the highest note of your range. Remember to pull that siren sound up to the high resonator at the bridge of your nose by tweaking the nose and keeping any strain away from the vocal cord area. You need to do your siren sound in full voice, so do not hold back. You must warm up at full volume. Remember, I did not say "loud," I said "full." Don't yell, but don't hold back either. The best place to do this warm-up is in the car with your windows rolled up. If you are in a hotel room or at home with other people in your house or apartment, you can warm up your voice without bugging your family or your neighbors. Just grab a nice thick towel and fold it double. Place it over your mouth to muffle the sound and start your siren blaring. Push down on that pelvic diaphragm to activate your alarm system (see Chapter 6).

Step 2: Avoid Emotional Stress

Emotional stress is the worst pressure you can put on your voice. Not only will it raise your pitch to an intolerable level, but it will also choke the muscles surrounding your vocal cords, causing a complete vocal blowout. Avoid situations that can suck the life out of your voice. If a confrontation arises before a presentation or any event that requires a strong voice, practice tolerance. Save your indignation until after you are finished with your performance.

Step 3: Chinese Headache Exercise

We enter this world inhaling a breath and we leave it exhaling a breath. Between those two events, wc sometimes forget how important a single breath can be, especially when we are speaking with increased volume. As I have said, breath is the lifeline to your voice, but for some reason, nobody teaches us how to properly breathe, unless we swim, sing, or study martial arts (see Chapter 6 to acquaint yourself with your breathing mechanism). Practice the breathing exercise below two times a day. Proper breathing is the fastest way to energize the body, next to caffeine, which dries out your vocal cords and won't help your voice.

This is an old Chinese breathing exercise I use not only to get my "pumpers pumping" and strengthen my breathing muscles, but also as a cure for headaches. It pumps the air through the body and fills it with a boost of oxygen. You'll love it:

- Stand with your feet slightly apart and your arms loosely hanging by your sides. Now begin pushing arms and hands backward as if you were moving through water.

- As you pump your arms, purse your lips as if sucking in spaghetti. Now suck in the air and blow it back out again as your arms tread back and forth through that imaginary, resistant water. Do this for one-minute intervals. You may get dizzy and lightheaded, as this will cause hyperventilation. (The dizziness will cease as your breathing power increases.)

Step 4: Practice, Practice, Practice

Speak or sing in front of anyone who will listen. Knowing your material and feeling comfortable in front of an audience eliminates self-doubt and improves self-confidence. Practice reading and speaking aloud with a confidant attitude—try out some of those voices you learned in Chapter 2. Remember, it is always helpful to do your voice work in front of a mirror so you can watch your facial expressions and body language. Create an effective voice for every occasion you can think of, and learn to change your voice as easily as you change the station on your radio. Don't be afraid to try something new. You may surprise yourself.

As you try out your new voice techniques in front of your mirror, be sure to add all three dimensions of your voice: depth for strength, width for variety, and length for projection. By using your entire body, eighty percent of the pressure is taken off the vocal cords and delegated back to the body where it belongs. This will keep those cords from shutting down and leaving you speechless in your hour of need.

Step 5: Take Good Care of Yourself

Your final step to preventing a vocal blowout is to keep your body healthy. The voice needs energy to survive and when the body is sick it takes every bit of available energy to fight the intruder, leaving the voice to fend for itself. It goes back to what we all know, but don't always do. To keep your body healthy you need to:

- Get plenty of rest.
- Eat a healthy diet.
- Watch your weight.
- Exercise.
- Avoid partying or overworking before the big event.

How you use your voice is up to you. You know what your voice needs, you know how to power it. Now, it's your call.

Check One, Check Two—Can You Hear Me Now?

There is one piece of equipment having nothing to do with your body that every professional singer must have, many teachers are beginning to use, and every woman who speaks before an audience should have access to, and that is a microphone/PA (public address) system. I have four of them and I guard them with my life.

There are several types. Some of them will make your voice sound warm and full with very little effort on your part, and some of them will make you sound like you're speaking down a tunnel. The larger the room, the more amplification you'll need. These systems come with four different microphone styles to choose from; some cost less than $200, which is less than a visit to the ER. (With a doctor's prescription, your medical insurance may even reimburse you for the microphone; if you teach, you may qualify for an educational discount.) For more information check on line for the current equipment available for speakers or visit your local music store. It is wise to seek professional help in choosing the best unit for your needs. When shopping for your unit, keep in mind that higher prices do not necessarily mean better quality.

Speaking Chic

How to Fashion a Voice Tailor-Made
for Your Message

Now that you are outfitted with all the information
you'll need to get your voice working, and you have
a good understanding of the unexpected perils that
can pull you off course, it's time to have fun, relax,
and go shopping for the perfect voice or—because there are many
to choose from—voices. You can pick a voice right off the rack
or be creative and fashion a voice that is a one-of-a-kind, designer
original.

With myriad voice choices, 37 and counting (see Chapter 2),
it is time to bring your unique, wise, and fashionable voice out of
the closet for all to hear.

The "Chic Revolution"

Chic means stylish, trendy, up-to-date, and classy. Although it is
generally thought of as a French word, it may have come from the
German word *schick*, meaning skill, fitness, and elegance. To suc-

ceed in business, this is exactly what a woman needs her voice to be: skilled, fit, and elegant.

If the 2008 political campaign taught women one thing, it's that no matter what words a woman speaks, if her voice is not pleasing to both men and women, there is bound to be criticism. When Hillary Clinton was calm, relaxed and informative, the media called her cold, unemotional, and detached from her audience. When she became excited and expressive, causing her voice to rise into that higher resonating chamber, they called her screechy and shrill. What's a woman to do?

Sarah Palin, on the other hand, mesmerized potential voters with her speaking voice. Unlike with Hillary, the media had no quarrel with Sarah's voice—she was a trained media professional and had been a sports reporter for stations KTUU-TV and KTVA-TV in Anchorage, Alaska. Sarah could be the spokesperson for why voice training is such a valuable asset for a woman on the move.

Articulation and Diction:
A Match Made in Heaven

First, let's clear up a big gray area before slipping into something more comfortable. When someone speaks of a voice that is muffled and inaudible, people often say that the person has poor diction. Actually, poor diction is not causing the problem; lazy articulation is. Although the two words, diction and articulation, are often used synonymously, there is a big difference that needs to be defined.

Diction refers to your choice of words. *Articulation,* on the other hand, gives meaning and feeling to the words you choose. Simply put, good diction is the choosing of strong, powerful, effective words and putting them together in a compelling sentence to stir and motivate your audience. Articulation is how you say those words, your tone of voice, emotion, and emphasis (especially on the consonants). Articulation is also the ability to move the mouth, lips, tongue, and teeth effectively so your words are clear and easy to understand.

Now that we have cleared that up, let's talk about words.

A Love Affair with Words

I love words. I love how they sound, how they make you feel, and what they express. Teaching my students the importance of the words they sing and speak taught me a huge lesson about the impact a lack of awareness or understanding has. "The Star Spangled Banner" provides a perfect example. When a singer, who has been asked to sing it at a sports event comes into my studio for help with the song, not only do some of them sing the wrong words, but when asked if they know what the words they are singing mean, few answer correctly. (It's ". . . the ramparts we watched were so gallantly streaming" that stumps most.) The point is, if the words you say or sing don't make sense to you, what you say or sing simply becomes blah, blah, blah—and the sound comes out of your mouth as meaningless babble.

Here is a challenge: Search online for the lyrics to "The Star Spangled Banner." First sing the anthem without looking at the words, then read them aloud. Now ask yourself if you sang it correctly or if you made mistakes. You may be surprised at the answer. Did you understand the parts you sang incorrectly? If not, look up the meaning of the words. Then the next time you sing them, you *will* sing the words correctly because you understand them.

When I read a book, hear a speaker, or listen to lyrics, I live in the words and rejoice when they move me. I am amazed at how good writers can assemble words that are magical to my ears and how other writers can use the same words in a different sequence and say absolutely nothing. Words are the incredible tools that we human beings use to communicate with each other. We can individually voice the same words in different combinations and create amazing poetry, lyrics, or one-line zingers. A few poorly chosen words in the wrong combinations can start a war, while a few well-chosen words, masterfully woven together, can end one. Words can hurt terribly, or make the heart leap for joy and change your life.

Voicing the Power of Your Words

When it comes to speaking and singing, used effectively words add power to your message and meaning to your song. When used ineffectively they can turn important information into a boring presentation. It all comes down to one major component—articulation: how you use your voice to express the words.

To speak with authority and command attention, a woman must become intimate with the words she speaks. Some words massage your vocal system as they pass through it and other words will feel uncomfortable and harsh. Some words have amazing impact on the listener while some are just fillers that take up space. Knowing the difference and making the right choices—diction—enhances the voice in the same way a fabulous piece of jewelry accessorizes the perfect outfit. When an accomplished actress like Meryl Streep or Dame Judi Dench says words like *cry, hard, soft, cold* or *hot*, their voices seem to become the word. *Cry* has a cry in it; *hard* sounds solid; *soft* is warm and fuzzy; *cold* has a shiver and *hot* has a bite. To learn how to get the most out of your words, you have to become, in some sense, a professional voice actress. Your job is to speak the words so your listener will not only hear them, but also feel and see them. It doesn't matter if you are speaking on the phone, one-on-one to your boss, in front of the entire company, or sitting at lunch with your spouse, each word should be a golden nugget of information that deserves and commands your listener's attention.

The word to write at the top of each page of your daily planner is "intent." What is your state of mind and purpose for delivering your message? In acting, it is called your "motivation." In business, it has called your "goal." To use your voice effectively, it always comes back to intent. Although you may be able to fool people with your written words, as they are subject to your readers' interpretation, the emotionally voiced interpretation of your spoken words is hard to fake.

Always ask yourself what is the reason or intent of your delivery? Is it to give information or to sell product? We have all been subject to the "hard sell" script, and no matter how benevolent the words, we can usually see right through them to the intent of the salesperson. If the speaker is a master of words, however, sometimes even the best of us is fooled, both professionally and personally. Once you understand that your goal is to make your voice more expressive and believable, your work is to choose words that match your intent and command attention. Words that are a good fit will feel genuine. The right words also have an actual physical effect on the body.

How to Punctuate Your Words with Your Lips, Tongue, and Teeth

Your lips, tongue, and teeth are called "articulators" because they are responsible for your articulation. They are powerful vocal tools. I love how some words vibrate my tongue, burble through my lips, tickle my teeth, and buzz my nose. As a singer and speaker, I have felt those physical vibrations pulsating through my voice and enhancing my melodic tone. Adding these three multi-talented parts of your voice to your breath, compressor, and resonating spaces can do fantastic things to strengthen and enhance the sound.

Every woman who has sung in a choir at school or taken some form of vocal instruction has done the "tip of the tongue, lips, and teeth" exercise to strengthen a lazy tongue and add flexibility to tight lips. And although when singing or speaking in English emphasis is usually placed on extending the vowels, it's the consonants that punctuate our words not the vowels. Vowels elongate the sound while consonants create definition with the help of your three articulators, the tip of the tongue, the lips, and the teeth.

Getting to Know Your Tongue

A lazy tongue creates lazy speech, so let's get that tongue of yours up and moving. Your tongue is more than meets the eye; in fact, the part you do see is only the tip of the iceberg. It's the part that is hiding underneath the tip, which, if not used correctly, can sink your vocal boat. Here is how it works: The tip of the tongue is directly involved in forming your bright sounding words. When the back of the tongue gets involved by rising up and blocking the hole in the back of your throat, your voice will still sound bright, but nasal. If your tongue pulls back toward the throat, your sound becomes dark and covered. If the tip of the tongue is lazy and weak, the voice is muffled and hard to understand due to poor articulation.

There are certain consonants that use the tip of the tongue and can keep it from pulling back in the throat and muffling your voice. (Stay with me here, please.) The consonants that keep the dark swallowed sound out of your voice are T, D, N, and L, which are formed by placing the tip of the tongue against the ridge behind your top front teeth. Go ahead, place your tongue up to your top gum line behind your front teeth and acquaint yourself with that spot. It's is called the alveolar ridge.

Here is my favorite exercise to help strengthen your tongue. Do it periodically throughout your day and keep at it until your tongue feels like a hammer pounding nails behind your front teeth on those Ds, Ns, Ls, and Ts.

Jump-Start Your Lazy Tongue Exercise

Run your tongue along the alveolar ridge behind your top front teeth. Now place the tip of your tongue on that ridge. With your tongue in place, say TA, DA, NA, LA (rhymes with ahhhh). Feel the tip of your tongue strike against the ridge to form the consonants. Using the tip of the tongue like a hammer, picture a row of nails along that alveolar ridge and begin hitting those nails with it while, saying TA, TA, TA, TA . . . DA, DA, DA, DA . . . NA, NA, NA, NA . . . LA, LA, LA, LA. Do this exercise whenever you can to strengthen the tip of that lazy tongue, but do not involve the jaw. This is a tongue exercise only. If your jaw insists on dancing up and down, hold onto your chin to keep that dancing jaw still. You will notice that the D has a much stronger sound than the T, which leaks air from each side of the tongue (hold this important thought for later).

Using the D, N, L, and T tongue position, practice the following sentences:

Don't do Dottie's dishes.

Dangerous dogs dig deep.

Never nestle near Nancy.

No neighbor needs to notice.

Let Lori leave later.

Little Leslie loves lettuce.

Twelve turtles take turns.

Take time to travel.

Awareness of Speech Patterns Exercise

Becoming aware of the speech patterns of your favorite female news anchors, actresses, women you work with, parents, friends, and all of those female voices you encounter each day is a great lesson in articulation. Listen for the pronounced Ds, Ls, Ns, and Ts. Be aware of the tongue's action and the part it plays in your vocal sounds, especially in your ability to be easily understood by others.

Do the tongue exercise to keep your own tongue wide-awake and strong when you speak. Watch how eagerly people will respond to a voice they do not have to work so hard to hear and understand.

Finding That "G" Spot Exercise

So much for the front of the tongue. Now let's move to the back where the G, C, and K hang out. Pick up your hand mirror, open wide, and with your tongue resting against the bottom gum line of your bottom front teeth say: GU, GU, GU (rhymes with uhhhh), and watch your tongue hump up in the back with each G and drop back down on the uh. Now say KU, KU, KU, and you will see the same action. Now try CU, CU, CU; note that the sound is identical to the sound of KU. Notice how just like the D and T, how much stronger the GU is than the KU/CU (again, take note of this for later). The G consonant is one of the stronger consonants bursting out of your acoustic hole from the back of the tongue. To strengthen this G action, stand in front of your bathroom mirror with your right hand holding your chin down while your mouth is open wide. Now watch the back of your tongue as you say, GU, GA . . . GU, GA . . . GU, GA. (again, rhymes with uhhhh and ahhhh). Again, the tongue humps up on the GU and drops down in the back on the GA. See how with your mouth wide open, using only your tongue, you can go from an uhhhh to an ahhhh without even closing your mouth or moving your lips or jaw.

Wag the Tongue Exercise

Every time you go into the women's room, take a few minutes to do this exercise. Stand in front of the mirror holding your chin down with your right hand so your jaw cannot move and say, GU, GA . . . GU, GA . . . GU, GA . . . GU, GA. Now reverse it and say, GA, GU . . . GA, GU . . . GA, GU . . . GA, GU. Do this at least four times a day to strengthen the back of the tongue.

Here are some G and K/C sentences to practice. Note how the Cs and Ks sound alike

Great games glorify gladiators.

Gossip gives Gracie goose bumps.

Keep coming closer, Kathy commanded.

Crispy cookies cooked with cream are keen.

Pucker Your Lips

Tight-lipped is a description no woman wants on her résumé. It immediately brings to mind a woman who is unbending and un-willing to share her information. To avoid that tight-lipped look, women spend millions on lip plumpers and various injections, which by the way are not only cosmetically attractive but also good for the voice. Tight lips can cause the voice to sound and feel tight.

One of the first exercises I have my female students do is blow air through their lips like a horse whinnying. To do this, let your lips flutter and flap in the breeze as the air (not sound) comes out of your mouth. You can do this exercise whenever you are in your car to keep those lips loose and movable. (It's much safer than talking on your cell phone while driving.) Don't get frustrated if they don't move the first time you try it. It takes practice, especially if your lips are tight. Those lips are the gatekeepers of your acoustic hole, namely your mouth. They can either let your voice come out or keep it locked in. Lips are also a big part of a woman's facial expression. We paint them red to attract attention to them, pout them when we are unhappy, and spread them wide when we are happy. Our lips tell everyone who we are and how we feel, and they play a big part in articulating sound. Nice, relaxed lips form a pathway for our words to come through, especially those that begin with consonant sounds like P, B, M, and W. To feel that lip action, put your lips together and say PU, BU, MU, and WU (the uhhhh sound of "duh"). Did you feel your lips move? Here is another exercise that not only keeps the lips loose, but also works the muscles all around them and keeps them full.

Burbling the Lips Exercise

Gently put your lips together in a relaxed pout and blow air through them just as in the horse whinny exercise. Starting with the Bs, blow the consonant sound through your relaxed lips. BA ... BE ... BI ... BO ... BOO. Now pop your Ps through your lips: PA ... PE ... PI ... PO ... POO. Please note that the B has a much more explosive sound than the P; the same is true of the D and the T.

Now try the Ws. I like to think of the W as a wind tunnel for the voice to travel down. With lips together in a pouted kiss position, say, WU ... WU ... WU ... WU (again, "duh").

The last consonant is the M. This sound is created using the buzzing resonators in your sinus cavity. It's bound to tickle your lips, your tongue, and possibly your teeth if you do it right (and that's a good thing!). Once again, close your lips, anchor your tongue behind your bottom teeth, pull the sound up your nose with a nose "tweak" and say MA . . . ME . . . MI . . . MO . . . MOO. When you elongate the sound using the breath, you are activating that third dimension of your voice, length. It is vital that your voice always moves out of your mouth, riding on that compressed laser beam of air, exploding out into the third dimension of your voice. Using your B, P, M, and W lips, say the following sentences aloud:

Betty brought bagels for breakfast.

Blue bobbles bring big bucks.

Put the puppy's paws in pink paint.

Pleasing places put Pam in paradise.

Walking with Walter works wonders.

When will Winnie want water?

More meat makes Mattie mad.

Maybe Monday Martha will make it.

Show Us Your Teeth

Anyone who has a dog is aware that when it wants to intimidate another dog, it will raise its lips off its teeth and snarl. It is called, "baring the teeth," and it adds volume to the growl. Baring the teeth also adds volume to the human voice. When your lips are covering your teeth, they muffle the sound. Lift them off your teeth in a snarl and your voice will automatically increase in volume. That's because sound bouncing against a hard surface (teeth) is clearer and sharper than sound against tight or loose lips. Lifting your lips off your teeth takes practice, so just think of your dog and snarl away.

- *If your voice tends to be shrill and cutting, let your lips relax loosely over your teeth to dampen the sound. If your voice is muffled and hard to understand, try lifting your lips off your teeth.*

Dental Workout

Your teeth do not work alone; they must be paired with either your lips or your tongue to do their job. The consonant sounds connected to the teeth are FU, VU, and THU (the "duh" sound yet again).

Placing your front teeth on top of your bottom lip makes the F and the V consonant sound. The F and V are called labiodentals because they involve the lower lip (labio) and the upper teeth (dental). Next is the TH sound, which is called linguadental because it involves the tip of the tongue (lingua) peeking through the top and bottom front teeth (dental). Let's put your teeth, lips, and tongue to work with this exercise:

Using the basic vowel sounds, A-E-I-O-U, place your upper teeth on your lower lip and say:

FAY FEE FI FO FU

VAY VEE VI VO VU

Now, let the tip of your tongue *peek* through between the top and the bottom front teeth like a snake, and while blowing air say:

TH (as in through): THAY THEE THY THO THU

TH (as in that): THAY THEE THY THO THU

Using your teeth, with your lips and tongue, speak these sentences aloud (remember to keep your front top teeth touching your bottom lip on the V and the F):

Funny faces feel fabulous.

Fine food from Finland tastes fresh.

Very versatile is Vera's voice.

Video violence is very vengeful.

Three thousand thirty-somethings think thoughts.

That was then; this is now.

Creating a Buzz

I love a warm, buzzing, resonant sound in a speaking or singing voice. It is like that sound you get when you have a cold and feel a vibrating tickle in your nose. It is praised in a singing voice and plays a very important part in creating fullness and warmth in a speaking voice.

It lives in the bridge of the nose and comes alive in the nasal consonants M and N. It can also buzz on the E vowel when it is pulled up high into the bridge of the nose.

To feel that buzz, place your index fingers on either side of the bridge of your nose and tweak (pull-up and wrinkle) your nose while humming like a buzz saw with your mouth closed. Or you can, try these exercises: wrinkle (lift up) your nose muscles as though you smelled something very bad. Say "yuk" as you lift your nose. Sneezing also pulls up the nose, so go ahead and fake a sneeze. Can you feel it?

Now with your tongue placed securely against your bottom gum line, say the letter M. Starting with an open mouth on "Eh" and closing it for the Mmmmm. Again, Eh–mmmmm. Now try an N sound. Begin again with an open "Eh," and keep your mouth open while pushing your tongue against the top gum line for the N. Say, Eh–nnnnn; again, Eh–nnnnn. Can you feel it? Here is a great exercise you can do in your car to get that buzzer started.

Buzzing the Ms and Ns Exercise

As you drive your car, read all of the road signs and billboards aloud. Now look for the Ms and Ns in those signs and pull them, buzzing, up into your nasal cavity. Buzz only the Ms and Ns; do not buzz any other sound, vowel or consonant. Here are some examples you can try:

> Farm-mm-ers Mm-market (tweak your nose on mm-ers in
>   farmers and Mm in market
>
> Turn-nn Right (pull up the nn with your nose)
>
> Are you getting the idea? Try another set:

> Mm-mayberry Mm-meat Mm-market
>
> Nn-no Right Turn-nn
>
> Nn-no Parkin-nng

After a few days of "buzz-sign reading," sneezing, and smelling, just the thought of an M, N will make your nose tickle.

Here are some M and N sentences to try with your new nose buzzers:

> Making a million mistakes means madness.
>
> Monday's moon must make Mindy melodramatic.
>
> Noisy neighbors are never nice.
>
> Norma's novel needs new names.

Once you have mastered the buzzing through the bridge of your nose, you can then add it to your ever-growing vocal repertoire of sound.

Define Your Voice with Captivating, Cool Consonants

Now, we are moving on to the major consonants that give definition to your voice. I have listed them according to the sounds they make when used with vowels. It is important to practice, practice; practice until your lips, tongue and teeth feel comfortable, strong, and happy to be part of your new effective voice(s).

You will start with the explosive sounds B-P-D-T-K-G—the consonants that explode out of your mouth by activating your tongue and lips. Using the a-e-i-o-u vowel sounds, repeat each line aloud two times.

Explosives: Use the lips and tongue positions described above.

BA BE BI BO BU
PA PE PI PO PU
DA DE DI DO DU
TA TE TI TO TU
KA KE KI KO KU
GA GE GI GO GU

Fricatives (sounds produced by forcing your breath through a constricted or partially obstructed passage in the vocal tract): Use your front teeth, lips and tongue.

FA FE FI FO FU
VA VE VI VO VU

TH (as in *through*): THAY THEE THY THO THU

TH (as in *the*): THAY THEE THY THO THU

Glides (sounds that come out your mouth on a beam of air): Use your lips and tongue.

WA WE WI WO WU

LA LE LI LO LU

RA RE RI RO RU

Nasals: Use your nose (sinus cavity), resonator, lips and tongue, and buzz away:

MA ME MI MO MU

NA NE NI NO NU

Powering Up Your Consonants to Punch Up Your Words

Now that you know your consonants live in your lips, tongue, and teeth as well as how to access them, it is time to put them to work. The consonants' job is to make sure your exquisite new voice is audible and articulate. When an actor is given an audition script and only ten minutes to look it over, the first thing she does is decide which words are important and should be emphasized. That decision will either make or break her audition. Many words have power and emotion built into them as we have discussed, but it is the consonants that give your words that extra kick.

A power word can start with a consonant or the consonant can come in the middle of the power word. Try it.

Punch Up the Explosive Consonant Exercise

This exercise will show you how to accentuate the consonants at the beginning of words. In particular, you will punch up (accent) the most explosive consonants, B, D, and G, and leave out the less potent P, T, and K. While reading these sentences aloud, look for the underlined consonants and emphasize them for greater impact. Note that not every B—or D or G—is underlined. This is because they are not key words to the meaning of the sentence. For example in "Don't *do* that." I chose to punch the word "do." You may choose to punch the word "Don't." The third choice is to punch both for greater impact. It all depends on how you choose to say the sentence. That is what is so powerful about learning to use the consonants effectively. How you choose to speak your words is always your call! Be sure to use your lips and tongue when appropriate, and don't forget to sneer and show your teeth. Punch away!

I *d*are you to *g*o!

Don't *d*o that.

*B*etter late than never.

He *b*locked her way.

*G*ive *b*ack the *b*ook.

That *b*ook is well *d*one.

What a *g*uy!

As you read each sentence aloud, it will become apparent why the Ds and Bs and Gs are my favorite power consonants for emphasizing my words and emotions.

Now let's add the Ns, Ws and Ls to the group and accent the underlined consonants in the beginning *and* the middle of the words. Here are your sentences:

It's *b*een an unpre-*d*ictable year.

Let's a-*b*andon the project and all *g*o home.

Your a-*b*ility is questionable.

She brings im-*m*ense responsi-*b*ility to the group.

He al-*w*ays *n*eeds the lime-*l*ight.

I'll say it a-*g*ain and a-*g*ain.

There is a *l*imit to what *w*e will liqui-*d*ate.

Next, write your own sentences or read the morning newspaper aloud, underlining the explosive consonants in the words you would like to accent. Remember the consonants you choose to "punch" can be at the beginning of the word, or in the middle of the word. Always use a pencil to mark your power-punched words because you may change your mind as you read your copy aloud. If it doesn't feel right on your lips, tongue, and teeth you can erase your first choices and select another group of consonants to accentuate. What you're looking for are the words that emphasize the key points of your message. If your audience hears your keywords, they can fill in the blanks and still get the point of your message, even if they miss a few words here and there. Choose wisely and give those keywords a good punch! While doing this exercise, turn on your recorder and listen to the expression in your voice. It will be very impressive.

Voicing Your Vowels

Although consonants still rule when it comes to articulation, vowels play a big role in fashioning your voice. Vowels are the sounds that elongate your words and add movement to your speaking and singing voice. Obviously, it's easier to elongate the vowels when you are singing and holding your notes, but vowels are just as important when you speak.

Consonants explode out of your mouth using the lips tongue and teeth; vowels glide out of the mouth on a beam of air with your lips and the back of your throat adding shape to the sound.

Vowels come in four shapes and two varieties. Two of the vowel shapes have rounded edges, which give the voice a warm, mellow sound, while the other two vowel shapes are square with sharp edges that give the voice a crisp, bright sound. The two varieties are the eight pure (single) vowel sounds and the five double vowel sounds, called "diphthongs." The dipthongs are commonly used in southern accents and country music while in jazz, opera, or big band music using a diphthong with two separate vowel sounds is an absolute no-no. Speakers, media personnel, and actors also avoid the use of the double vowel sound unless it goes with their personality or character.

Say AH . . .

The eight pure vowel sounds are:

Ah as in *all*.

Uh as in *up*.

Aa as in *can*.

Eh as in *bet*.

Ou as in *good*.

Oo as in *moon*.

Ee as in *me*.

Ih as in *sit*.

You may have noticed that missing from the list of pure vowel sounds are A, I, and O. That is because they are double vowels called diphthongs (see above). Those five double vowel sounds are:

Ah-Ee: I as in *night* (composed of two pure vowels, Ah and Ee).

Eh-Ee: A as in *day* (composed of two pure vowels).

Oh-Oo: O as in *hope*.

Ah-Oo: OU as in *about*.

Oh-Ee: O as in *boy*.

To try the diphthongs on for size, do the following:

Open your mouth wide and say, "Ahhhh" as if your doctor was gazing at your tonsils. Hold that Ah for as long as you can. While holding the Ah, smile wide, lift it up into your higher resonator, and listen to the Ah change to an Ee. By changing the shape of your mouth from an Ah to and Ee, your sound became an "I" as in ahhhheeeeeee.

As we continue, you will see how the shape of your lips can radically change the sounds you make as you speak. Practice forming those shapes with your own lips in front of a mirror and notice how the slightest movement of your lips can change the sound of your vowels and the tone of your voice.

An important difference between the consonant sounds and the vowel sounds is that the tongue has little involvement in forming vowel sounds. It rests against the bottom gum line and never leaves except to form the consonants D, T, L, and N, when it moves to the upper gum line. (I hope you have been doing your tongue exercises; by now, you should be able to move your tongue from the bottom gum line to the top gum line with ease).

Another difference is that although the shape of the mouth is constantly changing as we speak our words, the mouth is always open on the vowel sounds. The bigger the mouth can open, the bigger the sounds will be that comes out of it. Think of Mick Jagger, Jessica Simpson, and Jennifer Hudson. They all know how to open their mouths wide! The bottom line is, if you want to be heard in the back of the room, you must open your mouth on those vowels (this quality is often referred to as "open vowel sound").

Romancing the Tone

We all love a voice with warm resonant tones and when those tones are carried out of the mouth by well-shaped vowels, the result is magic. Consonants, on the other hand, disconnect the vowel sounds from each other by interrupting their beautiful tones and punctuating the words. A good voice has the perfect balance of both elongated vowels and punchy consonant sounds. A voice with too many vowel sounds has no personality and is often boring. A voice with too many strong consonant sounds is harsh and irritating and can make listeners uncomfortable. In fashioning your made-to-order, top-of-the-line voice, you will want to use them both wisely in balanced harmony.

Slowing Down the Motor-Mouth Syndrome

A statistic has been kicking around for years proclaiming that women use 20,000 words to men's 7,000 words. No one knows for sure where it came from or even what studies the figures are based on, but the statistics have appeared in numerous books and articles, and even some comic routines. However, recent studies show that not only do men talk as much as women, but they may even be outtalking us.

In my years of training voices, I have found that some women don't necessarily speak more words than men, but they do have a tendency to say them faster so that it seems like more words. When women speak fast, men have a hard time keeping up with them and miss half of what is being said. The problem is in the rapidity with which the words are said, not the words. Therefore, women with that *motor-mouth syndrome* need to slow down when they talk, and give the listener some time to process what is being said. When a woman speaks slowly, it gives her more authority and gives the listener time to digest her words and grasp her meaning. This eliminates the need to repeat yourself until your audience "gets it." Anyone who has studied acting has been told, "It's the space between the lines that makes the words come alive." In Acting 101, this is the first thing you learn.

Of course, the words are important, but it is the pauses between those words that not only help you slow your words down, they give the listener time to breathe. Think of each pause as the tick of a second hand on the clock and insert them into your speech and your voice personalities. That means all of your voice personalities—your telephone voice, your public speaking voice, your classroom voice, and even your mommy voice.

Here is an example of how to slow down your speaking voice that will be a lifesaver if you are prone to speaking even faster when you are nervous: "Hello (tick, tick) My name is Joni Wilson (tick), and I'm here tonight to tell you about your voice (tick, tick). But before we begin (tick) I'd like everybody to take a deep breath (tick, tick) and say hi to your neighbor (tick, tick, tick)." Try inserting those tick spacers into your everyday speaking pattern and you will find your audience, husband, children, and business colleagues hanging on your every (tick, tick) word. When the words come at you in rapid-fire succession, it is too much work to try to fill in the words you miss and much easier to mentally just turn the speaker off.

Speaking of being nervous, have you ever stood in front of a group of people with your heart pounding so loudly in your ears you'd swear the entire audience could hear it? Those throbbing beats are pulsating in your ears at approximately eighty-four beats per minute, as steady as a metronome. Rather than trying to stop those beats, which is a complete waste of time, take a moment before you begin your speech to tune into those beats, and use them just like the tick ticks to slow you down. When you are not resisting, your heart will begin to slow down, and you can settle into your natural speaking pace and be well on your way to a fantastic presentation. So don't panic the next time you hear that pounding in your ears; instead use each beat as a tool to slow you down.

Here is another simple exercise to help you adjust your pace.

The Metronome Exercise

Go to any music store and buy an inexpensive metronome. A wind-up metronome that ticks like a clock is perfect and portable. (Don't let them talk you into to any electronic, hi-tech model that bleeps and lights up—keep it simple. If you don't have a music store near you, you can go online and type in a metronome download for your iPod.) Next, find a nice quiet place where you will not be interrupted and set your metronome at seventy-two beats per minute. As it ticks away, practice your talk while staying within the beats. If seventy-two beats feels too fast, slow down the metronome two beats at a time (to seventy, then sixty-eight, etc.) until you find a pace that feels comfortable to you. If you go too slowly, your talk will be boring; if you go too fast, it will be hard to understand. When you find the perfect beat for your voice, write it down in you day planner and physically memorize the feel of it.

Next, grab the morning newspaper or your favorite magazine or book. Set your metronome at the perfect pace for your voice and read a chapter aloud as though you were reading to a crowd of fifty people. Remember to add your pausing ticks to keep your audience interested. When you feel ready, read aloud to your kids, your husband, your best friend, even your dog.

Keep practicing. Try out all of the techniques you have learned so far: breathing, phrasing, power words, punching the consonants, and the rest. When you feel brave enough, begin adding voices from your list in Chapter 2 to keep your listeners engaged.

Just the Facts: The Declarative Statement

The phrase "Less is more" is a good example of a short declarative statement. A declarative statement is a sentence that puts forth a fact. It is to the point and leaves no room for discussion. "It's hot in here." is a declarative statement. "It could be hot in here" or "It's hot in here, isn't it?" opens up the statement for discussion.

When presenting facts, avoid such qualifiers and questions as, "I think," "isn't it?" "could be," "maybe," "perhaps," and say it like you mean it. Just be sure you can back those facts up.

Forgo the Fillers and Say it Like You Mean It!

How we choose our words and structure our sentences brings us back to diction and the effective use of words to make a lasting impact on our audience. As stated earlier in this chapter, diction refers to your *choice* of words. Unfortunately, most of us use filler words not by choice but out of habit. As their name implies, filler words are words we use to fill up spaces when we speak. They can be whole words or just sounds. They are useless, can be annoying or disruptive, and are frequently habit forming (too often we don't even realize we've said them), and add no value whatsoever to your presentation. Obviously, before you can re-move them, you have to recognize that they are there.

What follows is a short list of the most common fillers beginning with the biggest offender, "uh." To familiarize yourself with this vocal parasite, begin counting the uhs used by your co-workers, friends, media people, politicians, and family members. You will be amazed at how epidemic its use is. "Uh" is followed closely by "um," "you know," "so," "well," "but," "okay," "like" and, the Valley Girl favorite, "like, you know." These words not only invade your speech, they invade your writing. I can go back over my writing five times and still find one or two embedded like fleas on a dog.

When Hillary Clinton first hit the campaign trail (I don't mean to "bag" on Hillary Clinton, but we've heard her so often, we can all relate to her), I was amazed at how many "you knows" came out of her mouth. I am sure somebody alerted her to that one, because as the campaign progressed, the number of "you knows" decreased. (If Hillary can do it, so can you.)

To add junk or filler words to a declarative statement weakens its meaning.

Returning to the statement, "It's hot in here," the key word is "hot." Now, what if you said, "I mean, it's like, well, you know, uh, hot in here, isn't it?" How effective and believable would that statement be? Of course, that is an exaggeration, but you get the point.

Filler Awareness Exercise.

1. Ask a friend to help you count your "uhs," "ums," and "you knows." (You can return the favor by counting hers or his.)

2. Record your side of your telephone conversations for a week. This time you are on filler/junk word alert. Listen to yourself. It could be a real eye-opener.

- *If an uncertain statement is voiced with authority, it tends to be more believable than the truest statement, filled with junk and filler words.*

Go Forth and Speak Chic

Now that you are outfitted with all of the information you will need to work the mechanics of your voice, keep in mind, when it comes to voice, one size does not fit all. Your voice has a style and uniqueness like no other. Do not be afraid to step outside the voice box and try on some of the voices you have been playing with as you fashion your perfect voice style.

((5))

Fear and Loathing of Public Speaking

How to Defeat the Jitters

"Why did I ever agree to do this? What was I thinking?" you keep asking yourself as you stand in the wings waiting for your introduction, but no answer comes. All the classic symptoms of a severe case of stage fright are invading your body and shutting down your senses. Your adrenaline is pumping and that "fight or flight" survival response keeps yelling in your ear, "Run now, before it's too late!" But it *is* too late—the host just announced your name and you're on . . .

You walk out on the stage, facing an audience of your peers, feeling like you've just stepped into a surrealistic dream. As you open your mouth to begin your presentation, every concept of time vanishes and, before you know it, your presentation is over. The audience rises to its feet cheering and a feeling of exhilaration is running through your body as you think to yourself, "This is why I was born. I knew I could do it." Completely forgotten are the fears and anxieties you felt so intensely thirty minutes ago. They're gone. Gone that is, until the next time you have to speak in front of an audience and the cycle begins all over again.

Staring Down the Stage Fright Monster

Some women feel about stage fright as some women feel about childbirth; each time they go through it, they swear they will never do again. When you think about it, placing yourself in front of a group of strangers and sharing your thoughts, ideas, and wisdom *is* like giving birth—the birthing of an idea. In both cases, there also is the anxiety that begins with an overactive imagination.

For the businesswoman, as the date for the next performance—audition, job interview, or concert—draws near, her anxiety revs up and she begins to worry: "What if it doesn't go well?" "What if it isn't perfect?" "What if my flight is late and I don't make it to the hotel on time?" "What if I can't fit into my expensive new suit?" "What if they hate me?" "What if I choke in the interview?" The list is endless.

Symptoms of Stage Fright

How much time and energy do we waste stressing and what-ifing? How many of those what-ifs will ever become realities? Most likely, none. That means it's not actually making the speech that is frightening, it's the *anticipation* of it—all the unknowns you feel you have no control over—that keeps your stress meter climbing and your fight or flight adrenalin pumping.

As a result, if you don't use it up by running for your life, it will show up as shortness of breath, a quiver in your voice, and a sense of impending doom. If you add to that a lack of trust in your own ability to handle whatever is put in your path, you have a very frightening situation. After all, women have been told for centuries that they are the weaker sex and should keep quiet. Even though we may deny it, there is still that small bit of history that feeds those seeds of self-doubt that are buried in the fertile soil of our belief system.

Still, it doesn't have to all be negative. Anticipation is a powerful source of energy that can be used in both a positive and a negative fashion.

Here are the classic symptoms of stage fright:

- Rapid heart rate (pounding in the ears).
- Shortness of breath.
- Uncontrollable shaking of hands and body.
- Nausea and stomach pains.
- Dry mouth and throat.
- Inability to concentrate.
- Feeling of impending doom in the pit of the stomach.

Stage fright monsters feed on our fears and our anticipation of a catastrophe, not on the probable, realistic outcome of our performance. Some of the most common fears are:

- Fear of judgment.
- Fear of losing control.
- Fear of forgetting your words.
- Fear the audience will laugh and boo you off the platform.
- Fear that you may not be as good as you think you are.

- Fear that you might pass out.

- Fear of someone saying, "Sorry, but you're just not good enough."

Stage Fright Is Real! Get Over It

When someone tells you "stage fright is all in your head," you can agree—to a point. It is in your head, but it's also in your voice, your body, and your nervous and digestive systems. It may start from imagined apprehension, but the symptoms that invade your body are real, and all of those affirmations posted on your refrigerator or dressing room mirror, denying the reality of stage fright are simply taking up space. Stop denying its existence, and step up and meet it eye to eye. The more you try to suppress your nervous anxiety, the more it will feed on your hidden feelings. Let the heart pump and the hands get cold and clammy and see it for what it is, your brain's instinctive reaction to your own overblown anxiety.

The way to overcome stage fright is to simply cut out the what-ifs and enjoy the challenges instead of fighting them. What follows is a list of some common what-ifs. Look them over to see how many of them you may have used to start your adrenaline pumping. Make a copy of this list and review it as you prepare for your next big event—singing or speaking. This will help you to get those deep, hidden what-ifs out in the open where you can challenge them and out them in their place. To personalize the list, add any other what-ifs that you have experienced. (There will probably be some overlap between your fears and your what-ifs.)

- What if I look like a fool?

- What if I forget the words?

- What if the audience doesn't like me?
- What if I lose my voice?
- What if I embarrass and humiliate myself in front of my family or peers?
- What if I pass out?
- What if I get sick to my stomach and have to leave the room in the middle of my talk?
- What if I just plain suck?

Consider this: what if you stopped resisting the negative energy and welcomed it by giving it positive feedback like, "What if I'm fabulous and everything I deserve is now coming my way?" or "What if they absolutely *love* my presentation and I get fifteen new clients?" Either of these should stop your negative, doom-and-gloom brain dead in its tracks. The emotions connected to a positive what-if will energize you to fight the negative ones. The point is not to buy into those thoughts of doom and disaster anymore. Keep them in perspective by changing your thinking and calming down the adrenaline. Instead of letting the anxiety frighten or anger you, try channeling all that energy in a more positive direction such as happily running through your presentation one more time. Emotion is a vital part of your energy and you don't want to lose it. An emotionless performance, presentation, or interview is boring, so your goal is not to put a lid on your feelings; your goal is to redirect those feelings in a more positive direction.

Changing the Way You Think About Stage Fright

It's always comforting to know that you are in good company when facing your demons, and, according to many studies, speaking in public is the number one fear of most people (men and women)—even greater than the fear of dying. Many of the finest performers and world-class athletes experience fear and anxiety before their performance. They call it stage fright but it's not the stage that is so frightening, it is the fear of inadequacy. Added to that is a lack of trust in your own abilities to perform to the standards *you* have set for *yourself*. They must be your standards because you have no idea what the audience expects from you until you have finished and they express their opinion by the way they react. If you set your standards too high—as many women have a tendency to do—you are simply setting yourself up for failure.

Enough said. Here are ten tips that will help you change your thinking.

Tip #1: *The audience is* not *your enemy.* They are there to hear what you have to say. They want your presentation or performance to be entertaining and beneficial so they don't have to sit through another boring forty-five minute talk.

Tip #2: *The more time you devote to preparation (rehearsal), the less anxious you will feel* about your performance, no matter what type is. Practice giving your talk in front of every object in your house located at eye level; your living room floor lamp, your dog, your husband, your kids, your best friend, or anyone who will listen and not criticize—your dog works best for that one. The point is the more you practice, the more confident you will be.

Tip #3: *Keep your presentation simple and entertaining* even if all you are presenting are the monthly sales figures. Don't bore your audience or you will lose them. A good rule of thumb is 70 percent content and 30 percent conversation or "comfort content." Help your audience feel safe. If they don't, they'll leave.

Tip #4: *If you are overwhelmed at the thought of giving a speech or presentation, create an alter ego* with a more aggressive personality than yours. Play with some of those female voices (see Chapter 2). When you can change your persona from afraid to unafraid and have fun doing it, your presentations will also be fun for your audience. That is always a win–win situation.

Tip #5: *Don't read your presentation word for word.* Even the best of actors sound "stiff" when they are reading a script. You can use notes as an outline, or PowerPoint, but try to keep your content conversational. Of course if you are reading a list, read it. No one expects a list to be entertaining, unless the person reading it is Robin Williams.

Tip #6: *Don't rely solely on the audience's reaction* to gauge the success or failure of your performance. You can't get into the minds of your audience, but you can control your own reactions. In other words, if you are having a good time, the audience will feel it and *join* you. The key word here is "join." The reverse is also true: If you tense up, the audience will feel uncomfortable. Some audiences are less demonstrative than others and even though they may not show it, they could be thoroughly enjoying your presentation. For years, I've had a recurring dream in which I'm on a stage singing and, for various reasons, the audience either gets up and leaves or is indifferent to my performance. Thank God, that has never happened to me on such a large scale in the real world. On the other hand, if it did, I'm ready because in my dreams I have actually worked through that sinking feeling of rejection, so I know that I would keep going and not end up a wasted heap on the floor. If you are secure in your material, audience reaction is a bonus, not a lifeline.

Tip #7: *They won't all be gems.* Even the best speakers, singers, and entertainers have bad days, when everything that can go wrong, does. Those are the times your nightmares become reality and separate the doers from the wannabes.

Every woman who stands in front of an audience must learn the fine art of "letting go." When the production is over, it is over, period. There are no do-overs or retakes in the real world. If you have a bad presentation, a dreadful audition, a horrible performance, or an embarrassing interview, give yourself twenty-four hours to grieve over what you "should have done," then open the door to the past, let that negative experience walk through it, and slam the door shut. Do not open the door and let it back into your thoughts. Let it go and remember, no matter how bad you feel when it's over—it's over!

Tip #8: Join a local Toastmasters group. It is one of the best places to practice speaking in front of an audience. It's inexpensive, supportive yet educational, accessible, and best of all, very safe. The only thing you need is a big cup of courage to go to your first meeting. Look up ToastmastersInternational.com on line and find a chapter near you.

If you're a singer, find the best "singer-friendly" karaoke club and get up there and sing. If you're a shy actress, join an improvisational group. Remember stage fright is simply performance anxiety. The more you perform, the more confident you become in your own skills and abilities, and the more at ease you will feel on the stage, platform, or podium.

Tip #9: Make sure your vocal skills are in place. If your voice is soft and weak, no one will hear your words. If your voice is shrill and annoying, people will stampede to get away from it. If your voice sounds too young, no matter how many PhDs you have tacked onto your name, it's hard to be taken seriously. Improve your voice and you will improve your life and your business.

Tip #10: *You are not afraid of a stage, you are afraid of* you. I'll say it again: Take control of yourself and the stage fright monster will stay locked behind that door to the past. The best solution to the problem is to face your fears as often as possible. Instead of avoiding situations where you have to talk, seek them out and speak to anyone, anywhere, who will listen. The more you put yourself out there, the more comfortable you'll feel.

Practice, Practice, Practice!

The best remedy for performance anxiety is to know your performance backwards and forwards—especially your beginning or opening. Know that opening three minutes so well you could do it in your sleep. Once you get past those first few minutes of panic, if you know your material well, the rest is usually smooth sailing. Practicing your material is the key. Rehearse and keep rehearsing your presentation until it is etched in your brain. Be so confident of your performance that nothing can throw you off. That is the best defense against performance anxiety—aka stage fright.

Stuff Happens: Prepare for the Unexpected

In a perfect world, every performance, speech, interview, or conversation with your boss about a promotion would end up just as you planned it. In the real world, there are some things you will never be able to control, no matter how perfect you try to be. Equipment fails, people are late, programs are snowed out, and flights are cancelled. That's just life; get over it!

Everyone should strive for excellence, because excellence is an attainable goal. To strive for *perfection* one hundred percent of the time is self-defeating and a waste of energy. I tell my students that when it comes to the voice, they should never expect more than an 80 percent return on their efforts and consider those very occasional 100 percent voice days a gift from heaven. Even Pavarotti, the most famous tenor in the world, once said, "If you have five good voice days in a month, you are lucky. The rest of the time you must sing as though you are having a good voice day."

If Pavarotti, who practiced five hours a day on his voice, could only claim five good voice days in a month, what does that mean to the rest of us? It means that we need to be more tolerant of our imperfections and our mistakes, because try as we may, we will never achieve perfection. Some of your performances will be better than others; a wise woman learns from her mistakes and is able to let go of the past.

"Accentuate the Positive"

Women are especially good at self-talk, I know I am. One of the most destructive things a woman can inflict on herself is the self-talk that goes on endlessly after she's made a big mistake or not lived up to her own expectations. There's no one more self-deprecating than a woman who believes she has let *herself* down. Women are, by far, their own biggest critics and judges. No one can make a woman feel as bad about herself as she can.

When a woman is down on herself, her voice is the first thing to go. A self-doubting female voice sounds whiny, weak, wobbly, and weary—not the voice that will take you where you want to go. You must reverse your self-talk from the demander of perfection to the supporter who loves you just the way you are, and accept every defeat as an opportunity to grow.

How to Boost Your Confidence

Below are eight things you can do—*must* do—to increase your self-confidence. A few of them are easy; all of them will bring you great rewards.

1. *Be prepared.* The more familiar you are with your material, the easier it is to eliminate those what-ifs, which are a major cause of performance anxiety. Practice in front of a mirror so you can see for yourself what your audience sees. When you like what you see, your audience will like it too.

2. *Find a stress reducer that works for you.* When my voice begins to tighten on stage, I open wide and give it a big yawn-sigh—"Haaaaaaaaaaaaaaa." Do not let your breath shorten into small gasps from the top of the lungs. Breathe deep from the bottom of the lungs (see Chapter 6). Air is the life force of your voice. Keep it coming!

3. *Visualize your successful performance.* If you can visualize it, you can make it happen. If you can visualize yourself triumphing in your interview with the boss, your presentation for the videoconference, singing on *American Idol,* or speaking in front of the entire company, you are on the right track to making it happen. Create positive, not negative, images of you up there "doing it!"

4. *Think positively.* No more negative self-talk to feed the adrenaline rush and start the cycle of stage fright symptoms. Your brain and your body will function better with a positive mental attitude. Focus on what you do well, not how you will "blow it."

5. *Keep a journal of the good things people say about you.* In my classes, I hand out evaluation sheets, which are filled out at the end of the class. I ask for opinions and feedback about my performance, my information, and anything I

can do to make the class better. When I received a negative review, it used to take me out of my comfort zone
for days—never mind the 86 positive ones. Now, I can
view the suggestions and silently thank the writer for
taking the time to give the opinion. I don't have to accept
the opinion, but I do appreciate it. If you receive any
comments about your performance, write them down.
Then write down what *you* think about your performance. You can be open to the suggestions of others but
what *you* think about yourself is what's crucial to your
self-esteem.

6. *Focus on what you do best, not what you* should *do best.* If
   your personality lends itself to humor, go for it. A well-
   placed laugh is a great tension breaker. If humor is not
   your thing, don't put yourself down because you can't tell
   a joke; find what you do best and be true to yourself. You
   cannot fool an audience into thinking you're good at
   something when you aren't—and no one is good at
   everything.

7. *Don't blow those little minor annoyances way out of proportion.*
   There is a book called *Don't Sweat the Small Stuff* by
   Richard Carlson, and I agree with Richard's point of
   view. Keep reminding yourself that perfection is not your
   goal. If you begin to beat yourself up for minor mishaps
   in the midst of a presentation, your audience will feel it
   and become uncomfortable, and when they are uncomfortable, they leave, if not physically then mentally.

8. *Be aware of your intentions.* Earlier we talked about your
   motivation. Why are you speaking, or giving an interview, or standing up in front of your entire company? Is
   your intention to be successful, to make money, to share
   your message with the world, or all of the above? Don't
   be afraid or think it is an ego trip to declare yourself a
   winner. It's Positive Thinking 101. If you can think it,

you can become it! To know your intent is to take all of the "what-ifs" and replace them with "I ams": "I *am* good at what I do!" "I *am* adding a lot to this company!" "I *am* the best CEO this company has ever had!" That list, too, can be endless!

How to Face Your Fears and Persevere

Fear is one of the nine emotions that can negatively affect your voice (see Chapter 7). Have you ever heard someone say, "I felt the fear rising in my throat"?

Fears to Confront and Conquer in Business

As a woman begins that frequently arduous climb up the ladder to success, she comes face to face with a number of lump-in-the-throat–causing fears.

Here are nine other fears that you may find familiar:

1. Fear of failure/fear of success.
2. Fear of making wrong decisions.
3. Fear of getting older/fear that it is too late.
4. Fear of losing control.
5. Fear of taking risks/fear of the unknown/fear of change.
6. Fear of abandonment/fear of being alone.
7. Fear of commitment/fear of betrayal.
8. Fear of money/fear of poverty.
9. Fear of work.

Of these, the fear of failure is the most destructive for any woman in business, especially if she's among the 51 percent of women who are sole providers for their families. Living with a fear of failure means you can never concentrate fully or do your best at work. Fear of failure can make a person afraid to state an opinion at the office even when her idea could save the company. Fear of failure can be so embedded that we subconsciously sabotage our own efforts so we don't have to continue to try. That's why many have linked the fear of failure with the fear of success. Failure is like a web spreading out from the center affecting every part of our lives.

As promotions pass you by, this fear can cost you thousands of dollars, damage your health, sabotage your quality of life, and rob you of your voice. Like most fears, the more you feed it, the stronger it becomes until eventually you fulfill all of your expectations.

To begin facing your fear, break each fear down into small, manageable pieces and handle them one at a time until you are comfortable. The first thing to do is find your voice. Try raising your hand to speak at the next sales meeting; try telling your boss about an idea you had to solve a problem. When you feel good about the small stuff, move on to larger risks.

A woman who fears success is usually soft-spoken and unaggressive. A woman who expects success has a strong voice (note I say "strong," not "loud") and is not afraid to use it to voice her opinions. Once you gain your voice, you'll find you are on your way to becoming that second woman!

((PART II))

Speaking "Up Close and Personal" with the Female Voice

((6))

Your Body, Your Brain, and Your Voice

Self-improvement books and motivational speakers are always urging people to think outside the box to create a much larger vision of who they believe they are. This is an excellent idea for creating a positive business image. It's also an effective approach to your voice.

To think outside the "voice box" is to think beyond that small area in your throat, the larynx (voice box), which houses those wondrous vocal cords that will soon become your new BFF.

When our voices get stuck inside the place that we affectionately call "my throat"—and we believe that the throat holds all of the power of our voice—the tendency is to push that voice way beyond its capacity to create sound.

Sound actually begins as a mere squeak in your vocal cords inside that voice box. Most of your voice problems are centered in the vocal cord/voice box area and are caused by trying to force those "squeaking" vocal cords into giving you one hundred percent of your voice power. This can never work, because your vocal cords are only responsible for 20 percent of your total voice

103

power; there's no way they can do what you so often demand of them.

To give you the strength required to be heard above everyday noise and clamor, your vocal cords need help from the rest of your body. This is especially true when it involves hour after hour of talking, singing, or shouting.

- *Fact: When you ask your vocal cords to do more than 20 percent of your voice work, they will simply shut down and take that much-needed vacation—often leaving you completely without a voice.*

It's very simple: your voice is just like all of the other parts of your body. When you push any part past its capacity to perform, the damage is obvious. Remember, your voice is a part of your body, and if you abuse it, you *will* lose it!

To have a rich, powerful voice that will last all day and carry to the back of the room, your entire body—which is responsible for the remaining 80 percent of your voice—needs to cooperate. In other words, to get one hundred percent use of your voice, you need to become familiar with *all* of the parts of your body that are involved in creating and powering the voice.

To begin, let's consider how your voice is actually put together. With that knowledge, you can get busy creating a voice (or voices) that will serve you well and last a lifetime.

Meet Your Vocal Cords

Let's start where your sound originates—those precious vocal cords that are responsible for all of the wondrous sounds that come out of your mouth. They create the high, middle, and lower tones of your voice, commonly known as pitch tones, or notes.

The vocal cords (or vocal folds, as they are technically called), are located side by side in your larynx (Adam's apple), and sit directly over the windpipe. Their primary job is *not* to create sound, but to close over the windpipe every time you swallow. This important function keeps you from choking to death while eating or drinking. Anyone who has ever tried to carry on a conversation at dinner while eating knows exactly what it feels like to get food stuck in the windpipe. For me it usually happens in a crowded restaurant when I'm eating and laughing at the same time. (Not a good idea when you are trying to impress a new client.)

To help you understand how this works and how it affects your voice, place your finger on your Adam's apple, and swallow. You'll feel the larynx rise to complete the swallowing process. If you talk or sing while the larynx is in that raised position, the sound will be strained and distorted, because to create sound you must now force those vocal cords to open when they are trying to close to keep your windpipe clear.

The Sound of Music

When they are given the right instructions, your two very talented vocal cords can create sounds that challenge the finest crafted musical instruments. Figure 6.1 presents a visual image of your vocal cords. (Note: The vocal cords actually sit over your windpipe in a horizontal position even though they appear to be vertical in the figure.)

Understanding Pitch in the Vocal Cords

Everyone who has watched the number one program on television, *American Idol,* has heard the panel use the word "pitchy" in referring to a singer's performance. The singing can be either sharp (above the correct tonal sound,) or flat (below the correct

Figure 6.1   The Vocal Cords

VOCAL CORDS
(Opened and Closed Position)

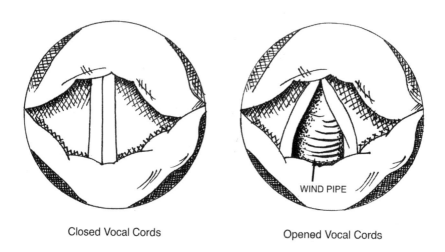

Closed Vocal Cords   Opened Vocal Cords

tonal sound). Either one can be called "pitchy," which spells disaster to a singer. To the untrained ear the song may sound just fine, but to the trained professional ear, "pitchy" is an abomination. To tune up your ear and help you avoid the "pitchy paradox," it's important to understand how pitch is created in the voice.

The variations in the pitch of your voice are centered in your vocal cords and are regulated by 60 powerful muscles lengthening, shortening, thickening, and thinning your vibrating vocal cords. Think of your vocal cords like the strings of a guitar. When guitar strings are plucked, the longer and thicker strings produce the lower, fuller tones and the shorter, thinner strings produce higher, thinner tones. The mechanics of your voice work in exactly the same way as the guitar strings. Using those 60 powerful muscles attached to your vocal cords, to adjust the length and width of those vocal cords you can create low voice sounds, middle voice

sounds, and high voice sounds, adding vocal variety to your singing and speaking voice.

- *Because the average male has longer vocal cords than
the average female—by around a quarter of an inch—a
man's voice will sound lower, thicker, and stronger than a
woman's.*

When It Comes to Voice, Size Matters

Big faces, big necks, big chests, big noses, big resonating chambers,
and big vocal cords, these are the natural tools used to achieve a
big, powerful voice. The very large female opera singer has been
saddled for years with the insulting, "It ain't over till the fat lady
sings." That overused indignity carries a big truth about the
human voice. When it comes to voice volume, bigger is defiantly
better. It is called the *girth factor*. (It's simply the dynamics of sound:
the bigger the speaker, the bigger the sounds coming out of it.)

The small singer/speaker with the big voice is always fun to
watch because she must move and push her body to get the big
sounds. If a singer doesn't know how to use her body as well as
her vocal cords, she is often plagued with voice problems
throughout her career. The same is true for a speaker, or for that
matter, a teacher, lawyer, salesperson, or any woman who uses her
voice to excess.

"Full" Versus "Loud": Speak from the Diaphragm

When it comes to vocal power, most women automatically think,
"How can I make my voice louder so they will hear me?" My
female clients are surprised when I tell them, "It's not a loud voice
you want, it's a full voice." These are two entirely different things.

Loudness lives in that 20 percent of the voice that comes from your vocal cords. Pushing and forcing them will create irritating, shrill sounds that annoy the listener, damage the vocal cords, and literally wear out the voice. Fullness comes from the remaining 80 percent of your voice, generated by using your body to power it, and creating those wide, resonate, warm, tones that are pleasing to the ear while massaging and strengthening the vocal cords. Learning how to access this power source to develop that strong, full voice without killing it takes practice, but is well worth the effort.

When I work with trained singers who are experiencing vocal problems, I always ask, "How do you sing from the diaphragm?" Usually, they point to their stomachs, which, in fact, house their lunches not their voices. Because your voice begins in your vocal cords, everything from the neck down has to do with *powering* the voice, not *creating* the voice.

What confuses them is the fact that there are two diaphragms connected to your vocal sounds, not just one, and it takes both of them to keep your voice working optimally. When you focus one hundred percent on the stomach area, you are ignoring half of your vocal power source.

The "Pump": The Abdominal Diaphragm

Like most parts of your vocal mechanism, the abdominal dia-phragm has more than one job to do. This diaphragm is located underneath the lower part of your lungs, and separates the bottom half of the torso from the top half. It stretches across the entire body and keeps the lower bodily fluids out of your lungs. That's job number one. Job number two is connected directly to your breath.

As you breathe in and out, the diaphragm moves up the top

half of the torso, pushing the air from the bottom of the lungs, up the windpipe, through the underside of the vocal cords, and out the mouth. Without this movement of air, you would have no voice at all. This diaphragm works just like a pump, pushing air out and sucking it back in again. Figure 6.2 illustrates your pump.

How the Pump Works to Enhance and Stabilize Your Voice

Because the air pressure outside of your body is different from the air pressure inside of your lungs, when the air is pushed out of your lungs by the diaphragm, a vacuum is created inside of the lungs. As the diaphragm drops back down to its resting place—sitting parallel to the second rib from the bottom of your rib

Figure 6.2   The Abdominal Diaphragm

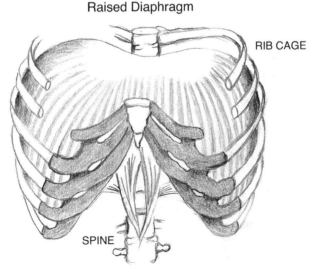

THE ABDOMINAL DIAPHRAGM FRONT VIEW

cage—that vacuum action sucks new air back into the lungs filling them to capacity. The wonderful part of all of this is, the diaphragm works automatically, and when you learn to use it correctly you will never again gasp for breath while singing or speaking.

To help you actually feel this pumping action, try my favorite "pant-breath" exercises. This will help you learn the fine art of "breathing while pumping your air."

The Pant-Like-a-Dog Exercise: Part 1

First, place your finger two inches below the sternum (breastbone), stick out your tongue and pant like a big dog on a hot day. You will feel the action of the diaphragm as it pumps air in and out of the lungs. When you first begin this exercise, you may feel a bit lightheaded. If so, stop panting until it passes, and then start again until your breathing feels effortless and free. With a little practice, your muscle action will soon take over.

Pump Up the Volume

Think of the action of a good, old-fashioned, bicycle pump. When you take it down from the shelf, the pump is always empty of air. You have to put that air back into it before you can pump any air out of it. You pull up the handle to fill the pump, and push it down to fill the tire. In other words, you must inhale air before you can exhale air, and to support your sound, the voice needs a solid stream of exhaled air to keep it steady.

Many of us breathe by lifting our upper body and filling the top portion of our lungs. This incorrect action stops the *natural* action of the abdominal diaphragm from filling the lower portion of the lungs. No wonder we have trouble breathing when we speak and sing. Using only the top of the lungs leaves us with an inadequate supply of breath in our vocal breathing tank. I always find it works better to separate the air we use to breathe and stay alive from the air we use to speak, sing, grunt, and do all of those sound-making things. So imagine you have *two* breathing tanks instead of one. One is filled to capacity, and when our brain tells us we are running out of air, the diaphragm automatically drops and sucks in the air it needs to keep you alive. It is one of those involuntary things we don't think about; we do it because our basic instinct tells us, "Breathe or die."

On the other hand, for tank number two to operate efficiently, it must be completely under your control. Short relaxed breaths are always your best bet for speaking or singing. Excess air forced up against the vocal cords restricts the flow of air and causes major "gripping" feelings in your vocal cord area.

To feel the abdominal diaphragm, here is a good awareness exercise.

The Abdominal Diaphragm Awareness Exercise

Again place your finger two inches below the breastbone and do the "pant-like-a-dog" exercise. The more you pant, the stronger the pumping action becomes. When you use your abdominal dia-phragm correctly, you can pump long breaths or short breaths de-pending on the length of your words and phrases—think big dog (long breath), little dog (short breath). In other words, you can pump the air as you need it, using the exact amount required for each task.

- This pump only *pumps* the air through the vocal cords; it does not power the air. Remember: The vocal cords create the sound, and air is the moving force behind that sound.

- To have a powerful voice, you need a strong, steady airflow.

So, if the abdominal diaphragm is not the power source of the voice, then where exactly does all of that power come from?

The Pelvic Diaphragm

You will recognize your second diaphragm as the power behind sneezing, coughing, and regurgitating; it also pushes babies and waste materials out of our bodies. In other words, it is the power behind everything that is ejected out of your body. Sneezes have been clocked at 100 miles an hour (Katrina reached 125 miles an hour). Imagine harnessing that power to push your voice up and out of your mouth. Your pelvic diaphragm lives at the base of your rectal area, as shown in Figure 6.3.

The pelvic diaphragm is one of the most powerful parts of the human body. You use it every day, and it knows how to do its job well. Surprisingly, the strength of your voice comes from the

Figure 6.3   The Pelvic Diaphragm

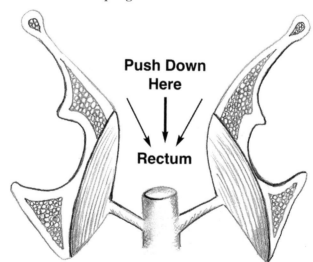

opposite end of your body than the sound comes from. Your vocal power source is about as far away from your vocal cords as it can get. For example, have you ever heard the powerful cry of a tiny, hungry baby? The more that baby pushed down on its tiny rectal area (plevic diaphram), the louder its voice, demanding food, became. That's a small example of the pelvic diaphragm at work. Now cough a good one and feel that downward "push". Now sneeze and again feel the pressure in the rectal area.

I tell my students who want power in their voices, whether singing or speaking, to push down on that pelvic diaphragm as if they had a very bad case of constipation. Not a pretty thought, but it gets the point across.

The Ho, Ho, Ho Exercise

Now that you know where the strength of your newly powered voice is coming from, it is time to put it to action with an exercise. This exercise will help you to gain control over both your pump— the abdominal diaphragm—and your compressor—the pelvic diaphragm.

Place both hands in the center of your abdominal diaphragm two inches below your sternum, at the spot where that diaphragm sits between your ribs. Now, say "ho, ho, ho" with all the gusto of Santa Claus on Christmas Eve. It's called a belly laugh, because the belly will bounce up and down when you laugh. As you say HO, HO, HO, push down on the pelvic diaphragm. Take another look at Figure 6.3—study it well. Feel that pushing down action and visualize that compressed air surging up the windpipe through the underside of the vocal cords and out of your mouth. You can control the air you pump by the amount of "push" on the pelvic diaphragm.

- *Always use the pelvic diaphragm to add power to your voice. It's like a built-in volume control that you can use as needed.*

When you need an extra burst of power in your voice, don't go near the vocal cord, throat area as that will only damage the voice! If you still can't feel that compression, try another cough or sneeze—that should do it.

The "How Strong Are You?" Test

If you have ever tried this test at a local county fair, you will instantly recognize it. The object of the test is to ring the bell at the top of the tower by hitting down on a metal plate at the bottom with a big hammer. The harder you strike down on the plate, the higher the hammer goes up towards the bell. You can take that concept and apply it to the voice, by imagining that the plate you hit with the hammer is your pelvic diaphragm, you *are* that hammer striking it, the clangor is your voice traveling up the vocal track, and the bell (the large resonating cavity at the bridge of your nose) is your destination. The harder you push down on the pelvic diaphragm, the more compressed your airflow becomes, and the more power you send up to your voice. The goal is to push down on that plate (pelvic diaphragm) as if you are giving birth to twins—both at the same time.

To test this, try pushing down on that pelvic diaphragm while cheering at your child's next big game or at any concert you attend. If you feel a pressure in the vocal cord area, try a stronger push. When it's is done right there will be *no* pressure on your voice. How sweet is that?

Power-Breathing Energy into Your Voice

To produce sound, the human voice needs two main ingredients, air and space. Without air, there would be no voice. The steadier the air flows up the windpipe and through the vocal cords, the steadier the voice will be. Think of your voice as lottery balls spinning on the top of a powerful pillar of air. If you turn off the air, the balls fall down. Just like those lottery balls, if the breath holding the voice up is not steady, that voice will also fall, causing an unsteady, unsupported, shaky sound. This quivering sound affects many female voices, especially when they are nervous, because women have a tendency to hold their breath and hyperventilate when they get nervous. This creates an erratic, unstable breath flow that in turn creates an erratic, unstable voice.

Learning to support the air is a prime-time lesson in voice control. Breathing correctly is a big factor in creating a powerful vocal sound, and to regulate and control how you breathe is to regulate and control your voice. To eliminate all the "shimmy dancing" in your voice, all you have to do is learn how to regulate your breath. It takes intention, practice, and the understanding that it is *mandatory* if you want to be the master of your voice.

There is a lot more to power breathing than just breathing in additional air. We have always been told, to breathe better, we need more breath, right? *Wrong!* There are times when it's just the opposite. Taking in too much breath can cause air to jam up against the underside of the vocal cords which, in turn, puts too much pressure on the vocal cords, constricting the voice.

- *Fact: The* steadiness *of the air being pumped through your vocal cords stabilizes your voice, not the* amount *of air being pumped.*

One of the big reasons for shortness of breath is breathing too much, which is an oxymoron to your brain. The answer to better breath control is not increasing the amount of air you breathe in; it is learning how to regulate your breathing.

I am always searching for faster, easier ways to build stronger breath support for my own voice. I have tried some bizarre exercises—all the way from laying on my back with books bouncing on my belly to holding my breath and hissing like a snake. Some methods worked, some did not. The books-on-the-belly bounce is very popular with voice coaches, but how often will you find yourself speaking or singing in that position?

The bottom line is the best thing you can do to achieve power in your speaking voice and improve breath support is to strengthen your breathing muscles and regulate the air you project out of your mouth. To begin strengthening those muscles, here is a simple exercise you can do in your car.

The Pant-Like-a-Dog Exercise: Part 2

Before you begin, let's review: The abdominal diaphragm pumps like a bellows, sucking air in and pushing it back out. The air pressure in the lungs is different from the air pressure outside of the body, so the pumping action is automatic. To breathe effectively, you must get out of the way and let the abdominal diaphragm do all of the pumping. With your tongue hanging out, start this pumping action by sucking the air in, and then panting it back out. In . . . out . . . in . . . out . . . Good! Now, once again, place your finger on the abdominal diaphragm and feel that pumping action. Pant fast (little dog), now slow (big dog), now medium (medium dog), and back to fast (little dog). Once again, you may get lightheaded; if you do, just stop and let it pass. As you become an accomplished pumper and begin regulating your breathing, the dizziness will pass.

The second part of this exercise is to add sound to the air. Remember that air is always comes first and sound is always second, riding out on the stream of air. Think of blowing a whistle, first comes air—blow—then comes sound—toot. Without air, there is no sound. Try it. Suck in the air and without stopping, add an "ahh-hhhhh" sound as you breathe the air back out. Don't pause as the sound goes back out on the ahhhhhhh. It's called a circle breath. This is exactly how you took your first breath as an infant, so your body already knows how to do this, and with a bit of practice you will know that it knows, and will trust it to do its job well.

- *Fact: If you put an H in the front of your ahhhhhhh (Hahhhhhhh), the sound will project further out of your mouth than it does when you say it without the H.*

When you get frustrated—and you *will* get frustrated—tell yourself, this is the way you were designed to breathe: in with the air, out with the sound. This is the natural way you breathe when you sleep, which means a third of your life is spent circle-breathing.

Your Brain and Your Voice

Remember the teacher who told you in fifth grade that you couldn't sing. Your brain is like a computer that stores information, and now every time you hear the word "sing," your brain digs up that annoying fifth grade teacher, just to remind you that you can't sing. Whenever that happens, say, "Thanks but no thanks," and dismiss the reminder.

Over the years, your brain has stored tons of information under the heading, "My Voice." That file contains every word, belief, failure, and triumph connected to your voice—along with a bunch of those myths we looked at in Chapter 1.

I am not saying your brain is the enemy, far from it. The main job of your brain is to keep you safe, to keep you from making a fool of yourself, and to keep you under its control. As you learn more and more about your voice, you'll discover that one of your biggest tasks is to dump the old voice software that is stored in your brain's computer. You need to get rid of what doesn't work and replace it with new thoughts. As your brain's main job is to keep you safe, you have to convince your brain that what you are doing is good, fruitful, and right for you.

If your brain cries "bull," it will not let you try anything new. Remember, in your brain, your safety comes first. So when your friends ask you to sing karaoke with them, and your brain starts digging up the fifth grade teacher, just laugh and tell your brain, "That was then, this is now." Don't let it win or you'll never experience the joy of finding your true voice.

Tip: Reread this chapter until you understand how your voice creates sound and your brain enthusiastically affirms, "Wow, that makes sense!" At that point, your body will automatically begin to do its part to help those precious vocal cords create sound.

((7))

Your Vocal Personality

Physical and Emotional Factors
and What to Do About Them

Nothing in a woman's day sucks the energy out of her voice more than feeling emotionally drained and physically tired. These two conditions can cause vocal stress and voice loss, when a woman needs her voice the most.

Women Who Wear Too Many Hats

According to the latest Bureau of Labor Statistics, nearly 60 percent of all women were in the labor force in 2005, and women are projected to account for just over half (51 percent) of the net growth in the labor force between 2004 and the year 2014. Today, more and more women are entering the work force and doing double duty, not only single women (the 51 percent of women now living without spouses), but married women who work all day and then come home to their second job of cooking, cleaning, spending time with their families, and trying to keep a normal family life going.

Although we women may think we have the DNA of Wonder Woman, the truth is, our female ecosystem is fragile and given the stress we put ourselves under, it's no wonder that we sometimes are worn out even *before* our day begins. All of this emotional juggling takes its toll on your voice, especially if your day job includes using your voice all day in a stress-filled courtroom, classroom, or office. By the time you get home, you don't have much energy or voice left to share.

The Dynamics That Mold Your Voiceprint

Every voice is unique with its own characteristics, personality, and emotional temperature. The voice can be analyzed with a tool called a sound spectrograph, and the graphic representation of the various frequencies representing these characteristics is called a voiceprint. Like a fingerprint, no two are alike. We also refer to the composite qualities of the voice (without the analysis) as its voiceprint.

My voiceprint was set in the fifties. My mother did not work, which was common in those days because keeping a household together was considered the woman's *job*. Like many women of my generation, I did not want that life for myself. I was caught in the "damned if I do, and damned if I don't" generation. I did my best to keep marriage, motherhood, and career together without feeling guilty, but despite my efforts, my two marriages still managed to fall apart. (Happily, my remarkable children managed to escape most of the fallout.) During my struggles, I never found the voice to say, "Now wait just a darn minute, this is not working for *me* and I need help!"

When you consider that it's only been a little over 50 years since women began to insist on having any voice at all, it's no wonder that so many of us are still willing to remain silent even when something is bothering us. Too many women still hate to make waves, cause problems, or muddy the waters, especially when it comes to the family, and especially after working all day. "Peace at any price," is the axiom of choice, but the mere act of constantly "stuffing" our voices deep down inside year after year takes its toll on our physical health, which in turn takes its toll on our voices.

Women's voices are often a blueprint of their emotions sitting out there, big as life, announcing to the world exactly how we feel no matter how hard we try to hide it. In my years of working with women, I have observed that the voice and the female emotions are joined at the hip.

When emotionally excited, a woman's voice pitch can go right through the roof. How many times have you heard a woman's voice described as shrieking, grating, high-pitched, or piercing? These adjectives are commonly associated with the voice of an overly emotional woman. I wish I had a dollar for every time over the past year someone in the media described a female voice with just those words. This is a *gender-based* statement frequently centered on a woman's response to an event. Being able to understand the effects her emotions have on her voice is a woman's first step toward learning how to control them, a skill every working woman needs in her vocal "toolbox."

Nine Emotions That Effect Your Voice

The following emotions can have a major effect on your voice: disappointment, frustration, happiness, sadness, anger, fear, self-doubt, love, and hate. These emotions can affect your voice by raising its pitch or its volume; causing constant throat clearing (more of a guy thing, but it also affects many women); creating shortness of breath; a harsh-raspy voice; a feeling of tightness or choking; nervous shaking; pitch breaks ("yodel" effect); breathiness; weakness; hoarseness; and everyone's worse nightmare, no voice at all.

The physical effects these emotions have on your body can also result in dry mouth, dizziness, lightheadedness, nausea, and lack of energy. Since stress at work and at home is the major source of most of these out-of-control emotions, the answer to this problem is to eliminate all of the people and things that cause stress in your life. Of course, this is easier said than done, and although there may be times when that sounds like a slice of heaven, the fact is that stress is here to stay. In terms of our voices, the best we can hope for is to understand what this emotional rollercoaster does to us, and take the necessary measures to get it under our control.

Let's look at those physical effects one by one, and explore some efficient ways to manage them better at work and at home.

Raised Pitch

When women get nervous, the pitch of their voices can rise dramatically. This is because the larynx goes into swallow position over the windpipe (see Figure 6.1 in Chapter 6, "closed" view). If you force the vocal cords to create sound while they are closing over your windpipe, they are pulled out of a relaxed (yawn-sigh) position (see Chapter 2) and put into a strained (swallow) position. To solve this problem you need to get that larynx back down into the relaxed position so your muscles can lengthen and shorten those cords and produce sound with ease.

To feel this action, place your finger on your Adam's apple, and drop your jaw into a big yawn-sigh position. Yawning the larynx back into a dropped jaw position releases the pressure on your vocal cords and brings your pitch down to a tolerable level.

- *You cannot yawn and swallow at the same time.*

To prove to your thinking brain that you cannot swallow and yawn at the same time, simply put your tongue against your bottom gum line, drop your jaw, open wide, and yawn. With your mouth wide open, now try to swallow. You will find that it can't be done.

Another way to keep your vocal cords in that relaxed position is by sipping water. By completing the swallowing process, the larynx will happily settle back down to a relaxed lower position. In addition, by preventing your chin from pulling up you will keep your voice from pulling up. This alone can instantly relieve pressure on your voice, even in the middle of your presentation.

Shortness of Breath

Shortness of breath makes us feel like we are hyperventilating. It is usually caused by breathing in short "gulps" with the top of our lungs. Many of us learned to breathe that way as children imitating the grown-ups around us. This action will only fill the small upper—instead of the larger bottom—portion of the lungs with air. When you are nervous and this begins to affect your voice, remember the pant-like-a-dog exercise (Chapter 6), and take a relaxed moment to focus your breath back to the bottom of your lungs. Let the abdominal diaphragm (pump) breathe for you. To keep your breath flow steady, don't hold your breath or try to speak long sentences without breathing. Just like any wind instrument (trumpet, trombone, flute, etc.), breath is the driving force behind your voice. That's why you must focus on deep breathing to keep the breath strong and the voice steady.

Harsh-Raspy Voice

That annoying harsh-raspy voice is caused by tension in the vocal cords and the voice sitting too low, putting pressure on those cords. This action results in a scraping, glottal sound, much like frying bacon—it is actually called "glottal fry" and it is very irritating to listen to someone who talks like this for an extended period.

If you suspect your voice is excessively raspy, place a small voice recorder next to your telephone for a week and record your conversations. This is an important assignment because women who have this habit can seldom hear it when they are speaking. The only way to fix it is to lift your voice off your vocal cords. In other words, speak in a slightly higher pitch. You may think you sound like Minnie Mouse, but no one else will even notice the change. (See Chapter 6 to learn how to raise the pitch of your voice.)

Tightness or Choking

Vocal tightness is usually centered in the jaw. Tight jaws equal tight voices! When we get nervous, the jaw tends to grip and grind the teeth, which causes that tight sound in the voice. The solution is to open your mouth, relax your jaw, and yawn-sigh a few times. A very wise teacher once told me that "chewing the days of the week" was also a great way to relax an overactive jaw. So start that chewing action while saying aloud, Monday, Tuesday, Wednesday; by the time you get to Sunday, your jaw will be totally relaxed. Try it; it works.

That choking feeling, on the other hand, is caused by a tight, raised larynx. It feels as though someone has you by the throat and you can't swallow. This can bring on sheer terror if you are in front of an audience when those grippers attack. The best way to handle this assault on your larynx and vocal cords is to drink water to jump-start the swallowing process. If the larynx stays in a raised position, your vocal cords will remain in a closed (swallow) position over the windpipe, keeping your voice tight and constricted. Keep water with you whenever possible, especially if you are a nervous speaker. Once you feel your larynx begin to move up, take a big chug and swallow (or yawn-sigh) that larynx back down to relaxed position.

Frequent Throat Clearing

This is a common problem for both men and women. This habit not only irritates the audience, it is very irritating to the vocal cords. This may be a nervous habit or the residue of a recent bout with the flu.

To solve this problem, it is important to understand how it originates. Mucus coats and protects the vocal cords, which are mucous membranes. When you continually clear your throat, you scrape off the mucus. In response, the body's defense system simply creates new mucus to protect your vocal cords. Anyone with a throat-clearing habit knows that the more mucus you clear, the more mucus comes flooding back in.

The solution to this problem is simple: In the yawn-sigh position, with your jaw dropped and relaxed, put your finger on your abdominal diaphragm and manually push the air up out of your lungs, through your windpipe and out of the mouth while saying "Hut . . . hut . . . hut" like a football quarterback in a huddle. You will feel the breath exploding up through the *underside* of the vocal cords, clearing out all of the debris (mucus) along the way.

Pushing air up through the underside of the vocal cords does not harm your delicate cords and eliminates their need to create additional mucus to protect themselves against abuse.

Nervous Shaking

Not only do your knees and hands shake when you are nervous, the part that shakes the worst is your *voice*. In singing, it is called "vibrato" when the voice oscillates up and down. In speaking, it is called "embarrassing" when the whole body shakes with nervous energy. Your best defense is to speak slowly because shaky, rapid speech is impossible to understand.

A shaky voice does not start in the voice; it starts in the body. As long as you are trying to stop your voice from shaking and not calming your shaky body, your efforts are totally misplaced. If you are standing in front of your peers shaking, find something to hold on to like a lectern (podium), a tall stool, a prop, just remember it is your body you want to calm down. Your voice will simply follow the body's lead.

Pitch Breaks (the "Yodel" Effect)

Like any chain with a weak link, your vocal chain also has certain areas in it that tend to be weaker than others. As your voice goes up and down (changing pitch levels) when you talk or sing—especially when you get excited—chances are you will be hitting one of those weak links in your vocal chain. When that occurs, the voice simply "yodels" over those areas, causing you to sound much like a young boy whose voice is changing or a country-western yodeler.

To avoid those pitch break areas completely is impossible. However, if you are aware of exactly where the weakness in your vocal chain is, you can add support to your words by pushing down on your pelvic diaphragm and compressing the air as it is pumped by the abdominal diaphragm (see Figure 6.2 in Chapter 6). Also, don't forget to breathe more often. As you run out of air support for your voice, the weaker links in your vocal chain become obvious.

- *To stabilize your voice, you must first stabilize your airflow.*

Breathiness

A continually breathy voice is a signal that you have a leak between your two vocal cords. It means that those cords are not coming together tightly enough, and that too much air is escaping through them. This causes the vocal cords to do twice the work they should be doing to create sound, which weakens the voice. A weak voice sounds hoarse and raspy and tires easily. If you are experiencing any of these symptoms, pay attention; it is the first sign that something is going wrong in your vocal cords. The breathier the voice becomes, the softer and weaker it will sound. A soft, breathy Marilyn Monroe voice may be considered feminine and sexy, but it diminishes a women's credibility in the business world, although it can be an asset to an entertainer. Many female singers have that raspy, breathy voice that sounds great in a recording studio but does not hold up night after night on a concert tour. When you have a leak in your vocal cords, you lose compression, and when you lose compression, you lose strength and power in your voice.

To strengthen those leaking vocal cords, you need to focus mentally on them. They live inside that fortress called your larynx; therefore, you cannot reach them physically to tighten them as you would a guitar string. You must send them a mental picture of what you need. Remember that the vocal cords work like valves to keep the hole in the cords that the air comes through small enough so the air will not leak. Pushing down on the pelvic diaphragm (see Figure 6.3 in Chapter 6) while mentally visualizing the cords squeezed in, can help strengthen your vocal cords.

Once you understand how to stabilize your breathing using your entire body, you will have better control of your voice even on the worst voice days. What good is an exercise if it only works when you are home in a safe environment? You must be able to control your voice wherever you are, whatever you are doing. I've learned to correct voice problems in the middle of a presentation simply by pushing down and compressing my air. As you become familiar with the feeling of a compressed voice, you will discover that this is an "inside job." No one can *see* you pushing down and compressing your air, but they sure can hear the strength in your voice when you do it.

Weak Voice

One of the major complaints I hear from women in business is that their voice is too weak and too soft. As you discovered in Chapter 6, it takes the entire body to move the voice up the windpipe and out the mouth, (it's that 20 percent voice, 80 percent body equation). By learning to activate the pelvic diaphragm every woman can instantly add power and volume to her speaking or singing voice. Projecting the stream of air on which the voice is riding out of the mouth increases the strength of the voice. I picture the air as a racehorse in full gallop, and the voice as the rider sitting on top of it. The power is in the horse (air), not the rider (voice). If a woman is asking her voice to do the work of the horse in this race, she will never win it! (This is a major complaint and is addressed throughout the book.)

Hoarseness or Complete Loss of Voice

Waking up the morning of a major business presentation or an important audition with a weak, raspy voice is a catastrophe waiting to happen. By taking the pressure off of the throat/vocal cord area, your voice—although it will not be one hundred percent—will, if used correctly, have enough power to pull you through the event.

A voice can also become constricted by the stress and pressure put on its owner to perform, even if it's just giving the monthly minutes at the company meeting. The fear of standing in front of the entire company can cause the larynx to rise, the vocal cords to close, and the airflow to choke off. The answer is to release the pressure on the voice by keeping the air flowing freely. Very seldom in all of the emergency calls I've received over my years of teaching has a voice been so damaged that it could not be coaxed back into active duty by removing the mental fears and the physical tensions in the body. Once you have experienced the wonders of a rebounding voice, speaking becomes less daunting and the voice becomes more trustworthy and manageable. (Stage fright is covered in depth in Chapter 5.)

As you read about the physical effects your emotions have on your voice, it should become quite obvious that if you are to have any control over your voice, you must first relax and stabilize the body. Your focus must be on the body's 80 percent involvement, not on the voice's 20 percent involvement.

Voiceprints and Voice Personalities

Every woman has a fingerprint all her own and that is part of her unique identity. Every woman also has a voiceprint and no two are alike. Along with her own unique voiceprint, every woman has an *emotional temperature* gauge, which molds and governs her particular voice personality. Think of it as body temperature controlled by emotions that can yo-yo up to boiling hot and down to bone-chilling cold in an instant.

Because your voice is closely connected to your emotions, and because those emotions can and, more often than not, *do* affect the sound of your voice, this invisible gauge is a dominant factor in molding your voice as well as your emotional personalities. The voice is your primary means of communicating with your fellow human beings therefore its effects on their opinion of you can not be denied.

A personality is defined as the complex of characteristics that distinguish an individual. A *voice* personality is that composite of characteristics that prompt us to regard some women as energizer bunnies and people magnets, while judging other women, who sit silently in the background, as having nothing important to say.

Where do these voice personalities come from? As children, we are great imitators; that's how we learn. Just as we learn basic skills, such as walking, eating, and relating to others from our primary caregivers, we also copy voice and personality traits. This is especially evident in second-generation show business families, where fathers and sons and mothers and daughters have strong voice and personality similarities. If the father's voice personality is aggressive and brash, the son often takes on his father's voice personality. If the mother has a baby voice, the daughter may imitate that voice, and as an adult, believe that her voice just sounds that way and cannot be changed. Nothing could be further from the truth!

Helping Your "Little Girl" Voice Grow Up

Because the voice is an instrument and you are the player, what your vocal instrument sounds like is *your* call, not some preordained family destiny. With a little work and understanding, every woman who chooses to do so can completely change her voice and its personality to one that better fits her occupation and personal lifestyle. No woman should be burdened with a voice that is not working for her. It is important to acknowledge that there is a voice actor living in all of us capable of playing many parts. Too often we are typecast in childhood and don't realize that we can break free from that image. See the list of female voices in Chapter 2 and explore your many options. Have some fun and try role-playing with those you like.

Voice Personalities and the Images They Project

Voice personalities come in many shapes and sizes. They can be positive or negative in business. Sadly, the women with an annoying voice personality is seldom aware of the adverse effect it has on her coworkers and clients. To put it simply, voice personalities are very apparent to others and often undetectable to their owners. For that reason, this section is essential information for every woman in business.

I recently attended a marketing seminar for women in business and the handout contained a list of voice personalities widely distributed to telemarketers and sales people to help them determine who will buy their products and who isn't worth their time. Each of these voice personalities also has distinctive traits and character-

istics that go along with them. As with the telemarketers, who are
only interested in making a sale as quickly as possible, our focus
here is on the problems each voice personality may create for a
businesswoman.

As you go through the voice personalities discussed below, see
if you can recognize yourself in any of them.

The Loud Talker

Unless the person has a hearing problem, the personality that ac-
companies a loud voice is often very demanding. This person must
be heard and may react aggressively when questioned. A loud
voice is a sign of wanting attention—and often signals a load of
self-doubt in a woman. Loud talkers love to hear their own voices.
They will answer their own questions while demanding your full
attention. They may sound self-confident but the underlying fact
is often just the opposite. If they can make enough noise, no one
will challenge them and discover who they *really* are.

The Soft Talker

A soft voice usually is attached to an unaggressive woman with a
perceptible lack of self-confidence. She does not speak up because
she believes she has nothing important to say. Such people often
can be easily led in their thinking by a more aggressive personality.
Soft talkers generally will not ask leading questions, and though
they may not agree with you, they usually will not question you—
just in case you are right and they are wrong. They are easily
intimidated, and rather than contradict you, they will more often
than not fold and go your way. I do not like to believe this profile
resembles me, but I was an unchallenging, soft-voiced person
when I was young.

The Fast Talker

People who talk fast often have a very active brain. Unlike the loud talker, who just wants to be heard and may take all day to make a decision as long as she remains the center of attention, a fast talker is there to get the job done. A fast talker is generally not a good listener and often misses the point. You will have to repeat yourself and be very clear in any of your business negotiations because a fast talker fills in the blanks then comes back a day later and swears that you agreed to do things you never even discussed. In dealing with a fast talker the rule of thumb—especially when it comes to business—is get everything in writing. Always remember the fast talker only hears what he or she wants to hear.

The Slow Talker

Slow talkers are generally very sure of themselves and often have an exaggerated sense of their own importance and your interest in what they have to say. When they are in control, they can drag out a conversation until everyone involved is exhausted. They never make fast decisions and need to know every detail before they cast their vote. They methodically weigh everything you say on a scale from one to ten. They are good listeners, but only because they need more information. Unlike the fast talker who often comes along to impress others, the slow talker comes to participate and truly believes that without their input, there would be no event.

Where Do You Fit?

Now that you have met them, did you recognize yourself in any of them? Obviously, the answer lies in the sound of your voice and your speech patterns. However, since you can't really hear your own voice or recognize your own voice personality, you may be the last to know if your voice is annoying. To begin the process of recognizing your own unique voice personality you can take the following Voice Personality Evaluation.

Evaluating Your Voice Personality

As you go through the following Voice Personality Evaluation, keep reminding yourself that you are not condemned to live out the rest of your life with voice traits and patterns that others may find annoying and offensive and you may find limiting. Keep in mind that voice characteristics are learned responses, which means you can *un*learn them and learn new ones.

For this evaluation, you need to enlist the help of your friends and trusted coworkers. Ask five friends or associates to pay attention to your speaking voice for five days. Remember, friends can come in all varieties and motivations so choose your participants wisely. It takes more than casual observation to accurately rate how you sound—it takes a good ear carefully listening for the predominant voice and personality traits. Five participants will give you a variety of opinions. I recommend choosing business associates to help with this evaluation rather than friends and family. You can even do it as a group "thing." Ask your associates if they would like to help you with your voice evaluation, and in return, offer to help them with theirs. As a bonus, you may even have a chance to help "fix" that coworker with the laugh that sounds like a cross between the Wicked Witch of the West and Scooby-Doo. That in itself would be a bonus for everyone in the office.

To begin your evaluations, do the following:

- Make a copy of the following Voice Personality Evaluation form for each participant and fill in your name at the top.

⦿ Ask them to pay attention to your voice for the next five days.

Remember when the evaluations are in, if all five people noted the same voice problem, that is a good sign that you need to pay attention to that area, even if you cannot hear it. Don't be offended by any of the suggestions, and don't change anything based on the opinion of just one person. Above all, remember this is a learning experience. (See the Voice Personality Evaluation on page 136.)

Dating and Your Voice Personality

Of course, we can't leave this chapter on the many things that affect how you come across to others without touching on how your voice affects your love life.

With Internet dating, relationships begin on the fast track; first impressions matter more than they ever did. We don't have time to *learn* to love someone any more. Today women follow life coaches and make lists of what they want in a relationship, so the "law of attraction" can get busy filling our orders. We take tests to see who will be a good fit for us, and with 51 percent of the female population now living the single life, the competition out there is fierce. Something is definitely wrong with this picture, but that's the world we live in.

Catching a Man's Ear Instead of His Eye

In the age of cell phones, speed dating, and "its just lunch," there are no do-overs when it comes to making a first impression. A woman has to "hit him with her best shot" at the first bell or he'll be moving on to the next table and she'll be stuck hanging out

THE VOICE PERSONALITY EVALUATION

The Voice Personality Evaluation for _____

Start date: _____

Below is a list of voice characteristics and speech mannerisms that you will be observing. Please note your comments in the allotted areas, and after five days, return this evaluation to the person you are observing. Be completely honest. Remember you have been chosen because of your objectivity and honesty. Thank you for your time.

Voice Characteristics: Rate from 0 to 10

_____ Too Soft—hard to hear and understand

_____ Too Loud—irritating

_____ High Pitched—irritating

_____ Lacks Emotion—boring

_____ Too Hyper—nervous

_____ Too Slow and Drawn Out

_____ Too Fast—hard to follow

_____ Monotone—boring

_____ Nasal

_____ Warm and Friendly

_____ Too Sexy/Breathy

_____ No Nonsense/Stern

_____ Businesslike

_____ Unbusinesslike—indecisive, uncertain

_____ Happy

_____ Angry

_____ Too Sweet—unbelievable

_____ Too Stern—unfriendly

Please complete the following statements:

I would like to do business with this voice because:

_____

_____

_____

I would not like to do business with this voice because:

_____

_____

_____

After carefully observing the voice of _____

over the past five days, I have reached the following conclusions (use the back if you need more room):

_____

_____

_____

_____

Thank you for your participation.

Your name _____ (optional)   Date _____

with the single gang on Saturday night. There are no second chances for a girl to make a good first impression anymore. She has to have the whole package ready to go, including her voice. You don't ever want to eavesdrop on a conversation that starts with: "How would you like to be married to *that* voice?"

Love relationships (even merely potential ones) can raise your emotional temperature and unleash those nine deadly emotions that have a negative effect on your voice.

- *A man's ear can be as sensitive as his eye when it comes to picking a mate*

Final Thoughts

The bottom line is, your uncontrolled emotions can affect your voice and tarnish your business and personal image beyond repair. These emotions can occur at the most inappropriate times, causing you to raise your pitch, cut off your breath, shake nervously, constantly clear your throat, experience dry mouth, or even completely lose your voice.

That's heavy stuff when your livelihood depends on a voice that sounds pleasant to the ears, especially when you are exploring a new relationship. Understanding the impact your voice has on your potential partner is vital. Whether it's business or personal, it's time to "get real" about your voice and how others perceive it.

((8))

Health, Hormones, and Heredity

This could very well be the most important chapter in this book because no matter how good your information is, how chic or trendy you look, or how many of those PhDs or MBAs you may have behind your name, if your voice is shot and you have to make a presentation, go on an interview, or impress a producer at the big audition, you've got a problem.

As I began this chapter on voice health, I was coming off a bout with the flu that took me out of my professional world for two weeks. For a person who is never sick and whose livelihood depends on a good, strong voice, it brought home a very important fact: taking care of yourself *before* you go down for the count is the best defense working women have against all the invisible thieves that can rob her of her voice.

I knew I had pushed myself to the brink in my work, giving myself no time to eat, sleep, or relax. I kept telling myself that I would do all that after I met my deadlines. Sound familiar? Luckily, my body was smarter than my brain and it mutinied, putting

everything on hold for twelve days, during which time I had neither the will nor the strength to do anything but lie in bed.

What does this have to do with *your* voice? Plenty. By ignoring my health and pushing myself past all reason, I missed my
writing deadline and three major presentations, and had to spend
the next month trying to catch up. Of course, we all get sick from
time to time and no magic pill that can prevent that. My goal,
however, is to alert you of some of the health issues that can affect
your voice so you can keep a watchful eye out for them and, I
hope, be smarter than I was and give yourself a day or two to let
your body regenerate instead of having it totally break down.

Major Health Problems That Affect the Voice

What you eat, how you think, how you keep your body's immune system in good working order, any medications you are
taking, family health patterns, sleeping habits, and routine illnesses
such as cold and flu, summer allergies, etc. . . . . all effect your
voice. In fact, you might consider your voice and throat area the
canary in the coal mine. More often than not, it rings a warning
bell that some physical challenge is about to come your way.

What follows are six everyday health problems that can pop
up unexpectedly, hijack your voice, and put a lid on a your well-
planned itinerary. Let's start with the one we all know best.

Colds and Flu

According to Medline Plus, which collects information from gov-
ernment and health agencies, in the United States alone, there are
more than one billion colds each year, and there is a very good
chance one of the billion will be yours. For some reason, this

annoyance always seems to hit on the date of your big presentation, audition, job interview, or opening night performance. I have watched this happen so often over the last sixteen years that I have been teaching women (and men, too) how to gain control over their speaking and singing voices when this happens. A cold or flu often strikes when a person is under pressure to succeed, so I also warn my students to be on the alert and follow their body's signals.

Facts and Myths

The common cold is the most frequent and elusive illness that affects the voice. Knowledge is the best defense against this relentless aggressor that can take you out of the competition in a heartbeat. Here are a few facts to help you understand the antagonist better.

There are over one hundred different cold viruses; of them the rhinoviruses are the most prolific and cause at least one-half of the colds we get. Rhinoviruses require living cells to reproduce, and they can only get to you when your hands touch your eyes or your nose, not your mouth. From the time the cold virus enters your nose, it takes eight to twelve hours to incubate and 32–72 hours for symptoms to appear. If you are on deadline, limit your contact with any known cold sufferers, especially during the first three days of their illness. Wash your hands after contact with anybody with a cold or after touching anything they may have touched. Most important, keep your fingers away from your eyes and especially your nose. Unfortunately, since people are asymptomatic for the first four or five days, this may not protect you enough.

The good news is that the voice can actually function in spite of a head cold because the voice is produced in the vocal cords and throat area, and nasal congestion from a cold or flu is produced in the nose and sinuses.

Those are the facts; here is the scoop on some common myths about colds:

Myth: Going outside on a cold, windy day with wet hair and sitting in a draft will lead to a cold."

Fact: Not so according to the scientists at the University of Virginia School of Medicine, who did an extensive study on the cold virus. They found that people who bundled up got just as sick as the people who were freezing cold, hence sitting in a draft does not give you a cold, it just makes you *feel* cold.

Myth: Once you catch the bug, you will become immune for the rest of the season.

Fact: Not true. The normal adult will get two to four colds a season and children will get twice that number. Interestingly, the older we are, the fewer colds we seem to get. The experts believe we have a cumulative immunity that builds up over the years.

Myth: If there is a cold going around your office, you are sure to get it.

Fact: No, again. Colds do not spread that easily at work. It takes direct contact with the virus to do the dirty deed. Remember, the virus lives on your hands and enters your body through you nose and eyes, so during cold and flu season, avoid touching your nose and your eyes if there is a chance you have touched anyone with a cold. All drugstores carry good antibacterial wipes so it might be wise to carry some in your purse. After my recent experience, and now that I know I can get this (or another) virus again, I too will be carrying wipes.

Myth: Kissing someone with a cold will give you a cold.

Fact: Hard to believe but the answer to that one is also no.

According to those experts in Virginia, the lining of the mouth is not friendly to the cold virus. If the noses swap fluid, you may transfer the virus. Cold sufferers are infectious for a few days before the wheezes and the sneezes begin. Your beloved may not even know he or she has a cold, so before you go nose to nose check out that canary in the coal mine (the throat).

Myth: You should feed a cold and starve a fever.

Fact: No one knows where that one came from. There is no scientific evidence that eating will cure a cold, but if it makes you feel better (and it well might), have a big bowl of chicken soup.

Myth: Menthol cough drops will help strengthen your voice.

Fact: If you are using your voice, avoid any cough or cold medication that contains menthol because your vocal cords are mucous membranes (as you now know), and membranes shrink when they encounter anything cold. For your vocal cords to function at peak performance, they must be warm and pliable. (Hence the importance of "warming up your voice.")

   The cool effect of menthol shrinks the vocal cords, causing the voice to sound thin and higher pitched. Check the ingredients in your medications and, if you will be speaking or otherwise using your voice, suck lemon drops to lubricate your vocal cords. If you're not speaking, presenting, or singing, menthol is just fine.

Knowing the facts is the best defense. Colds have a major effect on your voice, but knowledge about how to avoid them and what to do when they strike will help you keep the upper hand when they come to call.

Acid Reflux (Heartburn)

Ever since Ashley Simpson was caught lip-synching on *Saturday Night Live* and blamed an attack of acid reflux—which burns the underside of the vocal cords—for taking her voice away, singers and speakers have been using that excuse for canceling concerts and for voice loss in general. Laryngitis is no longer the favorite cop-out for voice problems. In the past two years, I have had a rush of students diagnosed with this rather new malady. Actually, it's not that new; it used to be called plain old heartburn.

Watch Your Medications

If the decongestant you are taking dries up the mucus in your nose, as it's supposed to do, it will also dry up the mucus around your vocal cords. Because those vocal cords are mucous membranes, they need mucus to lubricate them and give them mobility. The lack of mucus is what causes your scratchy throat, *not the cold*. Steaming the mucous membranes of the nose and throat with a few drops of eucalyptus oil—any health food store has it—works wonders. If you don't have a steamer, simply boil a pan of water on the stove, drop in a few drops of the oil, place a towel over your head and breathe in the healing steam all the way down to the bottom of the lungs.

There now is an assortment of new drugs to treat the problem. The only trouble is most of those drugs have drying effects on the vocal cords, which further antagonizes the voice. I am not saying that stomach acid is not real or that you should not get help when you need it, but in my experience, not every vocal problem attributed to acid reflux is actually caused by acid reflux; sometimes the irritation in the voice is caused by vocal strain, not stomach acid. In those cases, I am happy to say, good voice technique solved the problem and within a few lessons both the vocal problem and the acid reflux were gone.

Tip: If you are prone to stomach acid, try a mild antacid that will not have an adverse effect on your voice. Sipping a warm mild tea is very soothing for those overworked cords. (Throat Coat by Traditional Medicinals is my favorite.) Avoid foods that tend to upset a delicate stomach such as anything with caffeine or chocolate (sorry), and avoid acidic fruit.

TMJ (Temporomandibular Joint Dysfunction)

Your voice is an acoustic instrument and to give you its optimum level of performance, it needs to come out of a big acoustic hole. To put it simply, if you want your voice heard—open your mouth. I say those words repeatedly to women whose main complaint is that people do not listen to what they have to say. When a woman comes to me asking for more power and volume in her voice, one of the biggest obstacles standing in her way—like a sentry guarding the family jewels—is her mighty and powerful jaw.

The jaw has a mind of its own and like an unruly child, it decides when (and when not) to open up, regardless of your instructions. Many women fear that what they say either is going to embarrass them or is valueless, so they keep their jaw on red alert to snap shut at the first sign of indifference from their audience. With a quick "never mind," they simply shut up and remove themselves from the conversation.

What Is TMJ?

According to the TMJ Association, TMJ refers to a group of medical and dental conditions that affect the temporomandibular joint tissues in the area where the lower jaw connects to the skull. The symptoms include tight jaw, tension headaches, sounds of clicking and popping when yawning or opening the mouth. This is often accompanied by an intense fear that once that jaw snaps out of place, it can never be realigned. That is a major reason why many speakers, singers, and actors are afraid to open their mouths. Many things can cause TMJ, ranging from old sports wounds, auto accidents, braces, dental work effecting your jaw alignment, and crunching on hard ice—to cradling the telephone between the ear and shoulder.

The National Institute of Dental and Craniofacial Research (NDCR) of the National Institute of Health reports that over ten million people in the United States have some symptoms of TMJ and a large majority of those people are women. Women carry the tensions of the day squarely in their neck and jaw area and many women whom I have worked with, myself included, at some time in their lives have experienced mild to severe jaw problems. The words "tight jawed" are often used to describe a stern, no-nonsense kind of woman and years of tightening her jaw can cause a severe case of TMJ.

Retraining Your Stubborn Jaw

In my years of working with voices, I have found that understanding how the jaw works and implementing some very specific exercises will help to relieve stress and will teach that tight jaw how to relax. First, we have to let the jaw know exactly what we want it to do:

1. Open the mouth for food to go in and sound to come out.
2. Yawn so air can exit.
3. Chew.

All working parts of the jaw come together to achieve these three goals. When any of the parts refuses to cooperate with the others, the whole system must compensate for the problems that are caused, which creates an imbalance and pulls the jaw out of alignment. The goal is to teach your jaw how to realign itself so all its parts can work for the good of the whole. Before we begin, please study Figure 8.1 and get to know all of the jaw's working

Figure 8.1   The Jaw

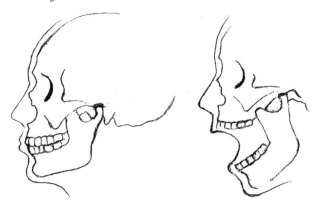

TMJ
(Temporomandibular Joint)

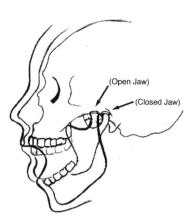

The Jaw Hinge Side View

parts; then do the exercises below to help you loosen up that tight jaw.

Retrain Your Jaw Exercise

Place your fingertips on both sides of the jaw at ear lobe level. Find the indented place that houses the mandible joint. Now, drop your jaw into a yawning position. The ideal jaw drops straight down and back. Do not allow your chin or your jaw to be pulled out of that dropped relaxed position or you will feel the jaw "pop" out of its ball joint (mandible) socket. When the chin juts or protrudes out as illustrated in the figure, the ball joint by the ear lobe will come right out of its socket. This action causes the larynx to rise up in swallow position, and the vocal cords to close over the windpipe, causing major voice problems.

Retrain Your Jaw Awareness Exercise

Watch how people around you open and shut their jaws when they speak. Notice how those with robust voices and hearty laughs, just open the mouth and "let 'er rip," while those who keep the jaw tense and tight, have tense and tight-sounding voices.

Buy yourself a small round shaving mirror with a stand. Set it on a table or desk in front of you and look only at the mouth area. Now, drop your jaw down into a full, wide yawn, hold it for three seconds, and *slowly* close your jaw. Do this several times, closely watching the up and down action of your jaw. Then ask yourself these four questions:

1. Does my jaw move forward instead of dropping down?

2. Does my jaw move from side to side as it opens and closes?

3. Do I stop before a full yawn for fear my jaw will lock outside of its socket?

4. Does my jaw do the "jaw dance" to the music of popping and snapping as it opens and closes?

While watching your jaws action in the mirror, slowly say "drop the jaw." As your jaw gently drops down on the AH sound in each word, dr—AH—p and j—AH—w, be sure to stay in the yawn position. Also, be very aware of how you close your jaw, and keep it in alignment; do not let it pull to the right or the left. Now say "mow the lawn," dropping the jaw on the O and AH.

This exercise will help you become aware of exactly how you drop your jaw, and then help you to correct the alignment of your jaw by slowly and gently training it to move up and down, not side to side. My own jaw had a tendency to pull to the right side when I closed my mouth because my mouth is crooked, as I have found most people's mouths to be. This constant pulling to the right not only interfered with my singing *and* my speaking voice, it also made my jaw very tired by the end of a long teaching day. I faithfully practiced the mirror exercise ten minutes a day for a month and corrected the problem.

Having that crooked, tight jaw also caused me to grind my teeth at night, often waking up the next morning with a very sore jaw. The dentist fitted me with a night guard, which solved this problem. It was one of the kindest things I ever did for my jaw. As the tension in my jaw lessened, my voice increased in strength and endurance. Correcting jaw problems early on eliminates many vocal tensions that might arise later in life. What you do now will last a lifetime, if you do it right and keep it up. Please be patient and remember those stubborn, old habits die hard.

Hormonal Changes and Your Voice

Hormonal changes occur in women of all ages. For some, the emotional effects can be so severe that all of the recognition and applause she receives can be overshadowed by an unexpected bout of sadness, despair, self-doubt, and vulnerability that seems to come from out of nowhere to slap her around for no apparent reason. Few women realize that these hormonal changes can also affect their voice throughout their entire lives.

The Young Female Voice

I have worked girls and boys going through puberty, guiding them during a time when their voices were completely unstable and undependable. The difference is that every young male knows that he will be going through a big voice change, one that traditionally is thought of as a rite of passage into manhood.

But nobody tells the young female that she will be doing the same thing, only instead of one big voice change, the female voice goes through three very subtle, smaller voice changes: one between 11 and 12 years of age, one around 15 and one between 18 and 19. At 11, none of us sounded like mature women, but something must change our voices somewhere on our path to womanhood because by age 20, our voice pitch has dropped considerably. Perhaps because this change isn't as dramatic in girls as it is in boys, we don't notice it or talk about it. This lack of understanding can often cause major voice damage in a young girl's voice if she tries to force it to sound like a mature adult woman's.

When you were in middle school, I'll bet you thought the annoying hoarseness that showed up sporadically was caused by yelling too loud at the football game, and laughing too hard with your friends. Or maybe you believed it was a cold you were catching from your best friend. You could always find a reason for the hoarseness even though it seemed to drag on and on and never go completely away.

What you were actually experiencing was a hormonal reaction to the natural growing process of your vocal cords. With an increase of estrogen, the cartilage and muscles of the larynx enlarge in size, and, as a woman matures, her vocal cords get longer and thicker. Remember, the longer the cord, the lower the voice.

While going through puberty and all of its body changes, along with the hoarseness in her voice, a young girl may also experience that *lump in the throat* causing her to constantly clear her throat to get rid of it. This habit can become so serious that it will follow a girl into her adult life, long after her vocal cords have adjusted. Remember, there is nothing in the throat to clear; you feel those 60 vocal cord muscles adjusting to their new length and position.

As that girl's voice grows up and becomes a woman's voice, it can actually drop in pitch by as much as four musical notes. Some girls will not have a mature woman's voice until their early twenties; until that time, they may experience periodic bouts with hoarseness and vocal fatigue as those cords grow and adjust. A young girl, who has no clue what is happening to her voice, can become very stressed when she is singing, talking, or performing, and can permanently damage her voice by pushing it too hard.

I have worked with talented girls who were ready to give up very successful acting and singing careers for fear their voices would not be able to handle the stress put on them by performing. Once they understood that all of the change is normal and natural and that it only takes a series of simple exercises to put strength back into their weakened voices, they gained a new respect for and confidence in their voice. It is amazing what vocal confidence can do for a young, budding career—or, for that matter, any of us.

PMS and the Female Voice

We all know premenstrual symptoms can bring on irritability, headache, bloated feelings, and pain in the back, but many of us do not know that PMS can also have a major effect on the voice. When the emotions take over, the body reacts and many women experience the emotional side effects of PMS. They may even experience the same hoarseness they felt at puberty because the larynx is affected by hormonal changes. Therefore, when estrogen levels drop prior to menstruation, water retention levels in the vocal tissues increase, creating mucus and hoarseness. Then, with progesterone levels on the rise, acidity in the mucus also increases, constricting the voice even further. It's an accepted fact in the world of opera that PMS not only affects the diva's voice, it can deplete her energy level as well, thereby hampering her perfor-mance. Most contracts with the divas have what is called a "grace-days" clause built into them, stipulating that she will not perform on those days. Wouldn't that be a great idea for every working woman who uses her voice?

Menopause

When a woman turns fifty, she is about to embark on the biggest hormonally caused voice "shift" she will experience in her life-time. This shift can occur during or after menopause. With less estrogen and more testosterone flowing through her body, the membranes covering the vocal cords increase in thickness, lower-ing her vocal pitch. In addition, the larynx may drop lower in the neck, again thickening the vocal cord and pushing her pitch even lower. As a woman's voice gets heavier and harder to move with agility, the natural tendency is to speak slower—it almost feels as though the voice functioning at half speed.

These hormonal events working together can cause the female voice to sound older and more masculine. It is sometimes called a "whisky voice" because women who have it sound as if they're spending their spare time in a smoke-filled pub. The good news is that this change can easily be reversed. In teaching women of all ages and backgrounds—both singing and speaking—I can honestly say that used correctly, a woman's voice does not have to age! When I make that statement in my classes, I am immediately challenged with questions regarding older women, whose voices so often sound wobbly, high-pitched, strained, and weak.

Consider this: Have you ever imitated a very old person speaking? To do this you have to tighten your jaw, grind your teeth, and shake your head to make your voice sound old and wobbly. In other words, you have to tighten and constrict the very muscles you use to create your vocal sounds. Those high-pitched, wobbly voices that some older people have are caused by years of abusing their voices with incorrect vocal technique or yelling, smoking, drugs (prescription or not), and toxic fumes, among others things. These abuses—alone or in combination— are bound to wear down and burn out your voice, in some cases long before you reach old age. I have personally helped 16-year-olds with strained and abuse voices that shook and wobbled more than the voices of my 70-year-old students.

- *With the right vocal technique and loving care of your body, your voice can become stronger not weaker with age. Your vocal cords may be delicate mucous membranes, but if you treat them with the respect they deserve, they will last you a lifetime.*

Voice Lift Exercise

It's time to put the zing back into your voice by giving yourself a good voice lift. To begin this process you must think *"lift."* Lift your heart, lift your shoulders, lift your face, lift your attitude, and lift your spirits, but do *not* lift your chin. (That will pull your larynx and your vocal cords out of position.)

It is best to do this exercise when you are completely relaxed, so here is a simple, relaxing self-hypnosis technique to calm your body and soul. Start by turning off your cell phone and locking your door.

1. Sit in a comfortable chair or on a pillow on the floor. Your body must be completely relaxed. Even the slightest bit of discomfort will distract you.

2. Now close your eyes, relax your face, and begin counting backwards very slowly in your head (not audibly):

   - 10—Take a deep breath.

   - 9—Feel your mouth begin to relax.

   - 8—Relax your lips, allowing them to feel heavy.

   - 7—Make sure that your tongue is completely relaxed and resting against your bottom teeth.

   - 6—Now drop your jaw in a yawn position and release all the tension from your jaw.

   - 5—Relax any tightness or tension between the eyes.

   - 4—Relax your closed eyes and eyelids.

   - 3—Relax your forehead.

At this point, all the tightness and tension in the face, neck, and shoulder area should be completely gone.

   - 2—Relax your head from the shoulders up. (This area should be a single completely relaxed unit.)

   - 1—With your lips closed, picture the biggest smile you can smile lifting your entire face to fit the smile. Picture the Joker from *Batman*, with a painted mouth from ear-to-ear. Now open your mouth and lift and stretch the corners to fit inside of that painted smile. Feel the entire mouth, soft palette (back of the roof of your mouth), hard palette (front of the roof of

> your mouth), uvula (that little dangling ornament at the back
> of your throat), and your teeth all lifted to fit that smile. While
> in that relaxed lifted smile position, say Hahhhhhh (big
> yawn-sigh)—ahhhhhh with an H on the front (Hahhhhhh).
> Then say, "Hi, how are you?" Now say, "Hi, my name
> is _____ (your name here)." Always let the air lead the
> voice out of your mouth by putting an H in front of the vowel
> sounds. (Reminder: As with any wind instrument, air is al-
> ways first, voice follows.) Now audibly tell all of your voice
> parts how light and free they feel: "My tongue is light and
> free." "My jaw is dropped and free." "My mouth is lifted and
> free." "My voice feels light and free."

Remember, your voice parts have no brain; they will believe what *you* believe. Believe in your new, free, lifted voice. It almost feels like you are about to giggle. Now open your eyes and find the nearest mirror. Look yourself in the eyes and give yourself a big, lifted (Joker) smile. Talk to yourself about how free your voice feels; be sure to keep your voice in that free lifted position. The more you do this lifting exercise the more it will become a habit and pull the heavy voice right off the back of your throat to the front of your face. As your voice becomes lighter and is more agile, it sounds young and full of hope.

After years of singing, speaking and teaching—sometimes six or seven hours a day—my voice is stronger than ever. I still sing with that big band, only now I don't try to outshout them. My voice is as strong after four hours of singing as it is at the beginning of the night.

Keeping Your Voice Young and Healthy

To go along with your voice lift, here are ten of my favorite things to do to keep your voice young and healthy. Copy the first sentence of each one and hang the abbreviated list on your refrigerator as a reminder.

1. *Never believe anyone who says the voice will weaken as you grow older.* Your voice mechanism has no brain; it only believes what you believe. To change the sound of your voice, start by changing your beliefs about it. Believe it is strong, powerful and made to last a lifetime if used properly . . . and it will.

2. *Include your voice in your daily exercise.* Do your abdominal diaphragm breathing exercise every day. Remember that the voice is a wind instrument; if your breath is strong, your voice will be strong.

3. *Drink plenty of water each day to keep the vocal cords hydrated.* A constantly dry throat causes dryness at the edge of the vocal cords. When relaxing, practice breathing through your nose instead of your mouth; this allows the air you breath in to become warm and moist before it reaches your dry vocal cords. This is especially helpful if you have to speak or sing in cold weather.

4. *Know how medications will affect your voice.* If you must take prescription drugs, always ask your doctor what side effects they could have on your voice. Any diuretic or decongestant, for example, is going to dry up the mucus that coats the vocal cords. If you know that, you can drink warm tea and suck on lemon drops to keep your voice from drying out and cracking when you speak. Remember to always avoid any throat medication or lozenges containing menthol. (Sugarless lemon drops will do just fine for the weight conscious.)

5. *Watch your posture!* As we grow older, the weight of the world seems to be pulling us down; they call it a "gravity thing." To pull it all back up, keep that area between

your rib cage and your hipbones lifted, especially if you are one of those women who sit at a desk all day. When the midsection is collapsed, the diaphragm is restricted and cannot pump, causing constricted breath. This not only allows your belly to "pooch out" but also stops the air from flowing freely up through the vocal cords. When the breath is restricted and shallow, the voice will be restricted and shallow.

6. *Be aware of the noise level around you.* If you find yourself at a Rolling Stones Revival Concert, do not, I repeat, *do not* try to outshout those huge speakers. There is rarely anything you have to say that can't wait until the end of the concert.

7. *Avoid continually clearing your throat.* Every time you scrape those cords together, you cause damage to your voice. It would be like constantly scraping the scab off a wound. If you do that day after day, imagine what that wound would look like in a week. Clearing your throat day after day can do the same damage to your voice.

8. *Keep your voice light and lifted,* especially if you feel depressed. Constantly speaking from the bottom of the throat weighs the voice down and causes the vocal cords to thicken, and thick vocal cords create rough-sounding voices in women. A youthful voice has that lift to it. Keep your spirits up. Think youthful and ageless and your voice will follow your thought. Honest!

9. *Take at least a half-hour each day to completely relax your body and your voice.* Never forget that your voice is produced by your body. Try a yoga class. Learn to meditate. Do the self-hypnosis exercise, or just take the time to sit in a quiet, beautiful spot and talk to no one. The voice holds all of our emotions and throws them back at us when we talk. To take a few minutes each day and not talk at all—

especially if you are a big talker—is the greatest gift you can give your voice. The voice can easily be affected by your emotions even when you are *not* talking, so along with don't talk, add don't think.

Drumroll please. Here is the most important thing you can do to keep your voice young and healthy:

10. *Don't smoke and don't drink alcohol in excess.* Smoking destroys the voice, we all know that, and alcohol is a dehydrator and will dry your vocal cords—a bit of social wine is fine but not if you are going to talk or sing within 24 hours.

Be wise and treat your voice and your body with the respect they deserve and they will be there for you your entire lifetime.

Chronic Laryngitis

One of the most overblown reasons for canceling concerts, speaking engagements and career building presentations is that ten-letter word that strikes terror in the hearts of women on the move: laryngitis. It has become the catchall buzzword for; "Sorry, I have no voice." We use the word repeatedly, but most of us haven't a clue what it is, how we get it, and how to fix it. To add to the confusion, there are six categories of laryngitis to deal with. Some are rare, some are common, but they all have a major effect on the voice. Take a quick look at each type:

1. *Infectious Laryngitis.* In this type of laryngitis, the larynx is infected with a virus, bacteria, fungus, or mold; it swells and turns red as the body tries to rid itself of the invaders. Most types of infectious laryngitis exhibit flulike systems

and are treated with antibiotics; those caused by fungus are treated with antifungal drugs.

2. *Contact Laryngitis.* This second type is caused by exposure to chemical irritants. Acid reflux is often included in this category, as are tobacco smoke, inhaled pollutants such as oven cleaners, paints, bleaches and hair sprays and dyes, and orally inhaled medications. The symptoms are a dry tickle in the throat, coughing, trouble swallowing, and sore throat leading to inflammation of the vocal cords and chronic hoarseness, huskiness, and complete voice loss.

   The treatment for this type of laryngitis is obvious: stop smoking and/or stay away from the chemicals that are causing the problem before extreme treatments such as steroid injections in the vocal cords and breathing tubes become necessary. This might be hard for women whose jobs depend on using chemicals, such as hairdressers, manicurists, and painters. If you are using harsh chemicals and your voice is affected, at least wear a protective mask. It may not match your outfit but it will save your voice.

   You can also soothe your inflamed throat with warm teas and throat sprays (without menthol if you are speaking or singing), and moisten it with water and lemon drops. If you continue to inhale toxic fumes, they will eventually take a major toll on your voice. Ask yourself if the abuse is worth ruining your voice.

3. *Mechanical Laryngitis.* I encounter this type of laryngitis most often. It is caused by vocal abuse and poor voice techniques, which force the vocal cords to go where they are not supposed to go. All of this yanking and pushing causes injury, swelling, and redness to the vocal cords. The result is chronic hoarseness, raspiness, and a complete voice loss. The treatment is simply to learn to use your voice correctly. Bed rest will relieve the problem for a few days, but the minute you overuse your voice again, the problem will return.

4. *Laryngeal Trauma.* This one, thankfully, is rare. It's caused by blunt trauma to the larynx or neck areas. Medical procedures such as intubation (placing a breathing tube down the airway), or inserting anything down the throat, even a tiny video camera may permanently damage your voice. Rest is the best medicine. Sometimes when the damage is severe; learning to redirect your voice and sound is the only fix. If this is your problem, find a good speech therapist or voice coach before permanent scarring takes place.

5. *Allergic Laryngitis.* Three out of five people who walk through my studio door have some form of allergy, especially children. Dust, pollen, dog, cats, mold can all cause allergic reactions affecting the voice. When allergies erupt and create histamine in the blood, mucus floods the sinuses. Everything itches, which causes sneezes and wheezes. This can go on as long as that histamine is in your system.

   The obvious treatment is to take an antihistamine, unless it's opening night and you have to sing or speak, because antihistamines will not only dry up the mucus but also dry up your mouth and throat. In working with my students, I have discovered that allergies can create a bigger fuller sound because mucus, like water, carries sound. If you don't take antihistamines, your voice should hold up for your speech or performance. A good steaming session with eucalyptus oil can also do wonders for the sinuses, and, during your speech or performance, make sure your water (as well as your tissue, if possible) is always handy.

6. *Laryngitis Sicca.* This is a strange one because it can be caused by any process that causes dryness in the vocal cords, such as dehydration, dry air from air conditioners and heaters, breathing through your mouth—which is what you do when you sing—and anything that can

dehydrate your vocal cords. This includes all beverages and medications containing caffeine. The only treatment for this type of laryngitis is to avoid the cause and keep your fluid intake high.

Nodules and Polyps

"Julie Andrews may never sing again following throat surgery." The headline was in every paper and TV news program in the country. Calluses on her vocal cords, commonly known as nodules, were the culprits. Nodules are noncancerous lesions on the vocal cords that result from straining and pulling those cords way out of their natural position. Nodules occur on both sides of the vocal cords, while a polyp is found only on one side. The symptoms are the same and often hard to diagnose. This is a common problem among older women and young girls, who strain to hit those "pop song" high notes. The symptoms include: a radical voice change, chronic hoarseness, and vocal fatigue; an unreliable voice (including a low, gravelly voice, low pitch, and voice breaks); delayed voice initiation (hearing your voice as if you were on a "digital delay"); an airy, breathy voice; the inability to sing high and soft notes; the need for increased physical effort to speak or sing; frequent throat clearing; and, sometimes, no voice at all. In other words, the symptoms include every voice problem imaginable.

Over the years, I have worked with women of all ages and professions who suffer from this condition to one degree or another and have found that with proper voice training, surgery—the traditional solution—can usually be avoided.

Stuttering and Lisps

A lisp and a stutter—or stammer, as it is sometimes called—can cause a great deal of stress, anxiety, and depression. Every working day can be a struggle with many embarrassing moments to endure, because those you work with—in and outside the office—cannot help but notice it.

Over three million Americans stutter, approximately one percent of the population. Stuttering affects four times as many males as females. Although there is no simple cure for stuttering, with speech therapy people who stutter can learn to speak more naturally and communicate more effectively. Stuttering typically starts between the ages of two and one-half and five. It's important for parents to seek an evaluation by a qualified speech/language pathologist as soon as any signs of stuttering are detected. Early intervention can prevent a lifetime of embarrassment and self-doubt.

According to the Stuttering Foundation, there are four factors linked to stuttering:

1. *Genetics:* Approximately 60 percent of those who stutter have a family member who also stutters.

2. *Child development:* Children with other speech and language problems or developmental delays are more likely to stutter,

3. *Neurophysiology:* Recent research has shown that people who stutter process speech and language in different areas of the brain than those who don't.

4. *Family dynamics:* High expectations and fast-paced lifestyles can contribute to stuttering.

Many adults who have stuttered all their lives may doubt that stuttering therapy can help them. However skeptical they may be, working with a pathologist who is knowledgeable about stuttering can usually help adults make positive changes in their communication skills. Finding the right speech pathologist and setting your goal to become an effective communicator should be your number one priority if you have this problem.

Stuttering therapy for adults usually means changing long-standing speech behaviors, emotions, and attitudes about talking and communication. Can a person who stutters still be successful? The answer is yes! Famous stutterers include James Earl Jones, John Stossel, Bill Walton, Marilyn Monroe, Carly Simon, and Winston Churchill. Some, like country singer Mel Tillis, find they do not stutter when they sing. If you stutter, you might give singing a try.

Living with a Lisp

Although I have not worked with clients who stutter, as this problem is best left to the speech pathologist, I have successfully worked with many clients, including speakers, singers, children, and adults—male and female—who noticeably lisp.

A lisp is a speech condition in which the "s" sound is pronounced "th" as in "the" and "z" is pronounced "th" as in "th-(z)ebra." A lisp can be barely noticeable, or very pronounced. Children with front teeth missing have a very pronounced lisp, which should give us a clue that our front teeth and the tip of our tongue are somehow connected with a lisp. Unlike stuttering, which may disappear when a person sings, a lisp is accentuated in the singing voice. Singing is simply elongated speech and when the "s" and the "th" are elongated, the lisping sounds are elongated.

I did not have a lisp until I had my two front teeth capped; the thickness of those newly capped teeth created my problem. It was an embarrassing time for me as a speech/voice coach with a speech impediment, but it was an amazing learning opportunity as I became my own student.

Tongue Strengthening Exercise

I was in the midst of recording voice lessons on tape and all I could hear on the playback was my very distinctive lisp. I discovered that the tip of my tongue against the extra thickness of my front teeth was working too hard and becoming tired and weak. It was too weak to stay out of the space between my upper and lower teeth. When that tongue was sitting in that open space between my teeth, all of my esses become th's. Try placing your tongue between your upper and lower teeth and say, "someday"; it will come out "thumday."

I began exaggerating my sssssss sound with my tongue anchored against my bottom gum line. Place your tongue against the bottom gum line, exaggerate your esses like a hissing snake and say "Sssssssomeday." This exercise helped strengthen the tip of my tired tongue. It soon became apparent that if my tongue was not resting between my teeth on esses and zees, there was no lisp.

This bit of information not only cleared *my* lisp, it has never failed to help my clients.

The Three "Rs" of Vocal Health: Rest, Relax, and Rejuvenate

The voice depends on so many parts of the body and if any of those parts, for whatever reason, become tired and overworked, the entire voice mechanism can be thrown out of whack.

According to NIDCD (National Institute on Deafness and Other Communication Disorders), some 7.5 million people have diseases or disorders of the voice. The good news is with the right information and training this number can be drastically reduced.

Your voice is one of your most important business assets, so make time in your busy day to give it the attention it deserves. Start with:

- *Rest:* The voice, like all parts of the body, can be pushed only so far before it simply stops functioning. To keep it happy and healthy, you must give it adequate rest. Don't allow it to go past the point of no return or no voice.

- *Even your voice occasionally needs some down time.*

- *Relax:* Stress and tension are the two worst enemies of your voice. Learning to relax your voice is especially important in the business world where most people spend the day with a cell phone glued to their ear trying to be heard above traffic noises, loud music, and the natural environmental clamor we live in. Try putting your cell phone down for an hour a day and *relax your voice.*

- *Rejuvenate:* After your voice is rested and relaxed, you can rejuvenate it by practicing controlled deep breathing, which will also help lower your blood pressure and slow down your heart rate. Using the pant-like-a-dog exercise (Chapter 6), combined with the voice lift exercise (earlier in this chapter) you can refresh, revive, resuscitate, and bring your tired voice back to life.

PART III

Falling in Love
with Your Voice

((9))

The Voice of a Winner

Putting It Together to Create the Voice of Success

n Part I, we talked about the tools you need to create your perfect voice—or voices—to deliver your message and advance your business career. In Part II, you learned about the complex way the female voice works, and we introduced you to all of the intricate parts that comprise your vocal instrument. You also learned how to avoid the many pitfalls that can challenge a woman's voice.

Here in Part III, you will find out how put all of this information to practical use, which will let you add the word *success* to your new vocal repertoire. When you close the final page on this chapter, you will have a new respect for your voice and its abilities.

Planting the Seeds of Success

Actualizing your "voice of success" requires some deep self-surfing and self-discovery. Although hypnosis, meditation, journaling, and goal setting are all effective ways of getting to know what you want, true success lies in the doing and being, not wishing and hoping. Without action, there is no lasting success. However, knowing what you want and visualizing the outcome are only the *seeds* of success, they are not the success itself. For those seeds to grow and be profitable, they must be planted in fertile ground, then watered with positive actions and tended daily. Your real work begins when the negative thought weeds pop up and try to choke the life out of your newly planted success seeds. Thoughts like "This takes too long." "I'm too old." "No one listens to me." "My voice is too weak." and the biggest self-sabotaging thought women have daily, "I'm just not good enough."

The words "overnight success" are also very deceptive. True success takes skill, and must be nurtured and developed. There are many types of success. For some women it is closing the multimillion-dollar deal to build a new shopping center. For another woman, success is finding the funding to build a skatepark for kids to use after school. Whatever your career or motivation in business may be, for you to achieve your voice of success you must first define your own unique talents and abilities. In other words, to be successful, you must first find *your* voice. Once you find your voice and know what you are passionate about, learning how to present it to others persuasively is your next step to success.

How to Find Your Voice

In many business classes and motivational seminars, teaching women the importance of finding their voice has become the metaphor for two major business challenges:

1. *Speaking up in intimidating situations.* This refers to the importance of voicing your thoughts rather than holding

them back. It's also about the need to understand the mental, physical, and career-blocking consequences that come from not speaking up.

2. *Getting your ideas across.* You've probably heard someone say, "I have finally found my voice." By this, the person often means she has found a way to express her ideas to others.

Speaking up is important, but missing from these seminars are the actual mechanics and voice skills needed to speak up and use your voice effectively once you've found it. Finding your voice is one thing, knowing how use it successfully in all business situations is another. Success is multifaceted and comes in many voices. Some of those voices help us to move forward in our careers and some of them cause us to take three steps back. We call those retreating steps "failures," but every successful woman knows that there is no such thing as failure unless she ignores the lesson it teaches.

Age Discrimination and Your Voice

When someone mentions age discrimination in business, most of us think first of an older person not being hired for, or losing, a job because of her or his age. Yet there is also discrimination against younger employees. A youthful voice can be as detrimental to a lawyer, teacher, executive, and saleswoman as an older-sounding one. A voice that sounds too young may not be taken seriously or cause employers and clients to doubt your experience and your skills.

Age itself is not always the problem. Sometimes it's not your actual age, but the way your voice sounds. In either case, it is the employer's or client's attitude towards age that is the obstacle.

Your job is to convince them that whatever their attitude, you have the skills and abilities to get the job done.

To do this you must create a voice to match your abilities. If your voice needs a more youthful sound, the exercises in Chapter 8 will help you accomplish that goal. Remember that your voice need not age, so do your exercises and give yourself a voice lift to keep it young and healthy for life. Lifting the voice is great for the older-sounding voice, but the younger voice needs fullness and authority. In Chapter 3, you learned how to access your 3-Dimensional Voice. The exercises in that chapter will help you sound more mature, more confident, more forceful. It's vital for your career to have your full voice under your control, no matter your age.

Stepping Onto Life's Stage: The Performing Voice

Up to this point, your voice has been approached from a purely physical perspective. You now know where the vocal sounds come from, how they work, and how to utilize all parts of your body for maximum results (see Chapters 2 and 6). The *sound* of your performing voice is only one part of the overall effect that makes your voice convincing and effective.

Some women are blessed with naturally beautiful voices. They can lull the audience into submission with the resonance of their voices and hypnotize them into conformity with its soothing to-nality. However, when the spell wears off, the presentation had better have content or no action will take place and business is action.

A speaking voice that has the authority to make people listen and then act utilizes these four components:

1. The sound of the voice itself.

2. Powerful content.

3. Energetic delivery.

4. Visual images.

All four are vital to gaining control over your business as well as your personal self-image. Without a strong self-image, it is difficult to convince audiences and clients to believe that what you have to say is valid.

The Sound of Your Voice

You can hide your shaky hands, but you cannot hide a shaky voice. Again, strong breath support and a good understanding of all your working voice parts are the two best remedies here. To give a good performance, you must know how to use the voice, how to master the fine art of phrasing and tone, the effective use of power words, and how to add color and vibrancy to your talk. You will find all that you need to achieve these objectives in Part I, Effective Communication.

Powerful Content

I am frequently amazed by speakers who believe they do not have to prepare a presentation, whether it was a business presentation or the after-dinner speech at a company banquet—or even the toast at a wedding. They think they are clever enough to just get up and say whatever comes to them, and that may be true if he or she is a gifted comedian like Ellen, or an eloquent orator like Maya Angelou, but even the best of the best know that preparation is the key to a good performance.

I know my subject, voice, backwards and forwards. I have been in the entertainment field all of my life. I have hosted talk shows, written plays, sung and spoken before large and small audiences, and I have even done stand-up comedy. Am I qualified to just stand there and improvise? *No way!* We have all, at some time, had to sit in the audience, listening to someone improvise with no direction and no point to their stories. After their presentation, they will even brag that they didn't take the time to prepare. Little did they suspect we already knew that.

Whether you are speaking one on one, or to a group of five hundred, to keep their attention, you must have something to say that they want or need to hear.

Forms of Presentations

Presentations are not one-size-fits-all. Knowing the kind of presentation you are making will help you design it to your purposes. Here are six of the most common types:

1. *Informative:* This is simply presenting a report or an update on the status of a business or company venture. It usually comes at the middle of a meeting and is short and to the point. Because it is usually repetitive and informal, adding a bit of humor or sandwiching some wise quotations in between the facts and figures can spice it up a bit.

2. *Sales:* This presentation is higher energy and more formal than the informative report. Its purpose is to persuade the listeners to take some form of action. Usually the action is to buy or sell more. It is based on the "Tell 'em, then sell 'em" format. Timing is everything in the sales presentation. You work the listener or audience into an excited frenzy, and then "nail 'em," as they say in hard sales literature. You can't be passive and do this kind of presentation well.

3. *Entertaining:* I have watched many a would-be stand-up comedian or "shower singer" fail at this type of presentation. If your purpose is to entertain, be sure your skills are polished and your material is clever and well timed. If you have additional talents—musician, singer, ventriloquist—you can weave them into your presentation. Whatever you do, be a professional. If you are an amateur, better stick to the speech or you could find yourself drenched in *flop sweat!*

4. *Training:* This type of presentation is a bit like lecturing in school. When people pay their hard-earned money to hear you speak, they expect something in return. It can be a half-day, a whole day, or a weekend session. To do this type of presentation, you must be an expert in your subject. You must be organized; it helps to have handouts, visuals, and to make audience participation a part of the event. If being up there by yourself makes you nervous, you can do a "buddy presentation." Bring in other experts who will enhance and add to your information.

5. *Motivational:* These presentations are designed to pump us up, make us feel guilty, feed us with positive energy, and tell us we have no limits. If the speaker is good, we believe them. Their presentations frequently contain stories designed to tug the listeners' heartstrings, which a good speaker will then pluck as if they were a precision instrument. Good motivational speakers are skilled performers! Women do very well in this profession if they have a good message and an excellent voice to deliver it.

Energetic Delivery

Woody Allen said, "Eighty percent of success is showing up!" That may be okay for Woody, but for the rest of us it doesn't work! After you show up and find yourself standing in front of your audience, whose eyes and ears are wide open, waiting to hear what you have to say, you need to be ready to deliver the goods. When that spotlight hits you, it's showtime, and you're on. The most frequently asked question is, "How do I start my speech and what can I do to grab the attention of the audience?" Your opener sets the tone for your presentation; if the opener flops, you might as well go home.

The average human attention span is estimated at 30 seconds or less. Therefore, you need to hook your audience right away or you will lose them. An average audience will take the first 30 seconds of your talk to go down their "let's check her out" list, which includes:

- The sound of your voice.
- Your physical attributes.
- Your attire.
- The intensity of your energy.
- How you move.

For the next 30 seconds they will focus on:

- Your delivery.
- Your attitude.
- Your speaking skills.
- Your subject matter.

If the audience is still with you after the first minute, you are well on your way to success. That is, of course, unless you drop the ball and bore them with dry, long-winded material.

You have to start by jolting the audience to attention. Characters, jokes, stories, and other gimmicks work well for the big entrance. In Chapter 2, I listed 37 voices. You have had the opportunity to play with them, so by now you should be ready to launch into a lucrative career as a "voice-over" talent (well, it would be nice . . .). At the very least, you should have a good idea of just how versatile your voice can be. The catch is there has to be some reason connected to your presentation material to use those voices or tell that story or the entire effort will fall flat on its face. Let's go back to the big question, "How do I start?"

One way to start your talk is to activate the brain cells of the audience by asking them a thought-provoking question, and then show them how only you have the answer to that question. For example, ask your audience, "How many of you would like to be debt-free in five years? Raise your hands. I'm going to give you the formula today to make that a reality in your life!" That sounds like a Suze Orman opening, but for a woman in finance that type of question is a great attention grabber. If you're a health expert, here's a good question for a group of women: "Would anyone here like to lose 20 pounds while eating all of the foods you love? Show me your hands. Good! Tonight, I'm going to show you how to do just that!" Whatever the subject, starting with a good question involves the audience from the get-go.

Another approach is to shock the audience with frightening statistics. This is a more in-your-face approach. As you stand center stage, take a moment to look your audience in the eyes and calmly and slowly deliver a shocking fact, such as, "Every day millions of working women are exploited on the job . . . and they don't know what to do about it!" A lawyer speaking to a group of homeowners might open with "Fifty thousand lawsuits are filed every day! You could be the next one sued and lose everything you own!" Those are fun and you can find all of the shocking facts and statistics you need online. Just type in your subject and be as creative as you can be.

If your talk is on the gentler side, you may want to start with an appropriate quote from a famous or historical person. You can find quotes on everything from the Bible to Shakespeare to the latest hip-hop sensation. Today there are many books filled with quotations on just about every subject by anyone who has ever uttered a sound. There are CD-ROMs for your computer filled with quotes listed by categories, and there are free websites offering quotes. Quotations make good opening statements and are excellent icebreakers for novice speakers. An appropriate quote can also be very effective in a formal business presentation. Good examples are "Shoot for the moon. Even if you miss, you'll be among the stars" (Anonymous), and "The first step you should take if you want to be successful is to decide what kind of executive you are. Executives fall into three categories: those who make things happen, those who watch things happen, and those who wonder what happened" (John M. Capozzi). If you know whom you are quoting, give the person credit, if it comes without attribution, you can say, "I heard this wonderful quote yesterday that really made me think. It was . . . etc. etc. etc."

Can't you just see yourself standing up at the company business meeting with all eyes turned to you, starting your presentation with the perfect quote, or maybe even telling your own story?

Visual Image: Body Language and Your Voice

Whether we like it or not, when we are standing in front of a group for that first one minute, they are visually taking us apart. This does not mean that you need to be young, thin, and attractive to be successful. It's important, however, that your visual image fits the presentation, job interview, business atmosphere, or special occasion that you are representing.

Most women are very perceptive when it comes to knowing how to dress. If you have any doubts in your own abilities, invest in a good image consultant to help you. What eludes most of us is our own body language. Unless our presentation is videoed and we have the courage to watch it, most of our quirks, twitches, and body movements pass us by, unnoticed. Because your body is 80 percent of your voice, how you use it is crucial to your voice image as well as your visual image.

"Do You See What I'm Saying?"

I used to get irritated when someone asked, "Do you see what I'm saying?" "That's ridiculous!" I would think to myself, "How can I *see* what you're saying?" Then I began to notice how important body movements were to a speaker's and a singer's performance. The body tells a story of its own, regardless of the words that are said. It is as if a nonverbal conversation using the eyes, hands, feet, the direction the body moves in, and the entire upper and lower torso is going on. They don't call it "body language" for nothing.

The San Diego Chapter of the National Speakers Association did a professional video taping session for its members. Twenty-two professional speakers participated. Each one took a ten-minute segment out of their talk to use as a video demo. I was one of the 22 speakers. The session started at 9:30 A.M., ended at 6:30 P.M. and I was last! I had to sit there all day watching speaker after speaker make their best shot. As a voice coach, I paid particular attention to what did and did not work for each of the speakers, not as a critic, but as an observer. I was fascinated listening to all 21 voices, each one entirely different from the other. Some were strong and authoritative, while others were soft and timid. It soon became obvious that the stronger voices also had a tendency towards strong body movements.

Early in my vocal teaching career, I learned how important the arms and the hands were in adding power to the singing voice. It is also true of the speaking voice because the vibrations of your body have a powerful affect on your voice. A strong fist pounding, even in the air, will cause the voice to vibrate. That vibrational movement in the body and the voice will add punch, volume, and energy to your words. Posture and arm movements are very important to your overall visual as well as vocal image.

One of the biggest frustrations for an inexperienced speaker or singer is what to do with her hands. I tell my students that the hands should always look natural while enhancing the meaning of the words. Planned hand, arm, and body movements can look fake and stiff if they do not go with the words that you are speaking—or singing. All power words (see Chapter 4) have a natural movement to them.

A good rule of thumb that I use to help clients find workable hand and arm gestures to go with their words is this: If the sentence applies to any element or person outside of yourself, the arm and hand movement is outward and away from your body. If the word or sentence applies to you, your thoughts, or your emotions, the hand and arm movements are inward towards your body.

- *For gestures, remember: "Inner (self), inward; outer (other), outward."*

Not only does the body affect the voice, it also affects the audience's perception of you, and how they actually hear your voice. How many politicians have you seen who appear stiff in their delivery because their body movement is not natural (especially that pointing finger)? You must move! You cannot stand like a stick. But you can't pace like a lion in a cage either. Find a happy medium that works best for you. Remember, one movement does not suit everyone. We are all individuals. Use what works and feels best for you and your total image.

Videotape Yourself

Practice speaking in front of a video camera using all of the voice techniques you have learned so far including:

- Punching the buzz words (Ms and Ns).

- Marking appropriate dramatic pauses in your text.

- Marking the beats for phrasing.

- Controlling your breath.

- Adding power to your voice by using your two diaphragms.

- Using your 3-Dimensional Voice power system.

Look for the emotions in your words and let them guide your hand and arm movements. Try different movements and don't be afraid to experiment. If a movement looks stiff and unnatural to you, it will look stiff and unnatural to your audience.

If you don't have a video camera, you can use a full-length mirror. But if you're serious about public speaking, business presentations, coaching and classes, or media and job interviews, a good video camera is essential for helping you perfect your presentation by watching your most vital asset at work, namely: your self.

Finding Your Business Voice

Your business voice is part verbal communication and part state of mind. You won't succeed in business until you believe in yourself enough to transform your thoughts and ideas into actions. Whether you are the owner of your own business or moving up the corporate ladder in a Fortune 500 Company, there are no limits to your success except the ones you put on yourself. You may argue office politics, gender and age discrimination, economic hardship, and all of the other reasons you can find for not succeeding, but those arguments are no longer valid; there are too many successful women out there who have overcome the same blocks. If you need inspirational stories to motivate you, there are hundreds of books written by women who found their voices and put them to good use.

Successful women are not afraid to take on a challenge. If they don't have the specific skills it takes to do the job, they have enough confidence in their ability to learn the new skills that they don't let a good opportunity pass them by.

The Voice of Reason: Speaking Up

Sound judgment and the ability to persuade or influence using the faculty of reason to reach conclusions is a huge asset in the business world. The businesswoman who can back up her suggestions with indisputable facts and solid reasoning is certain to gain the respect of her coworkers and the attention of her employers. Add to that the ability to present those facts with a competent voice, a self-assured attitude, positive presentation skills, and a willingness to toot her own horn loudly, she will sink the competition.

If you want to move on, move out, and move up the career

ladder you must not only create value in yourself, you must demonstrate that you know your product and your message well. We live in a knowledge-based world that is performance-driven. With information so readily available online, if you don't do your homework and get your facts straight, your credibility will go down in flames. With so much competition for high-level jobs, the days of faking it and getting by on your looks or personality are gone, and if you "blow it" there are very few second chances.

Men often have a greater sense of their own worth—warranted or not—and there are those who don't hesitate to speak out even when they don't know what they are talking about. Women, on the other hand, in many business situations, still have to prove themselves. Because that burden of proof is still on us, it is imperative that a woman on the move keep her facts reasonable, credible, and accurate.

With many men still questioning what women are doing in what was once their exclusive club, it is no wonder women sometimes question themselves. If you doubt your own abilities, it's hard to promote your unique values. Yet promoting yourself is a key item on the power agenda. When you are competing for a promotion, if you don't mark your territory, you can end up lost in the corporate jungle. Use your voice of reason to:

- Be visible.
- Be bold.
- Be factual.

Those three "be's" will help you win the promotion and also give your career a great jump-start!

The Voice of a Leader: The Lead Dog Always Has the Best View

A leader is a groundbreaker, initiator, trailblazer, pioneer, and trendsetter. Women are joining together, widening that path, and walking down it side by side instead of in tandem. More and more women are finding their voices, accepting leadership roles, and taking risks than ever before in our history, and it seems to be getting easier. I recently saw the movie *Iron Jawed Angels*, which tells the remarkable and little-known story of a group of passionate and dynamic young women, led by Alice Paul and her friend Lucy Burns, who put their lives on the line to fight for American women's right to vote. This tenacious group of women endured horrific physical torture and ridicule for the right to have their voices heard. It makes any struggles we have today look like child's play. To be a leader takes courage, a tenacious will to succeed—and a voice to which people want to listen.

A leader must get used to being in the spotlight, which means it's time to prepare your voice for media interviews, lectures, speeches, book tours, audio books, instructional DVDs, online video classes, etc. If you are to be a leader, you are going to need your voice of success running at peak performance.

((10))

Singing Your Way to a Better Speaking Voice

Before you shake your head and say "Why would I read a chapter on singing? I don't sing," consider this; learning to use your singing voice offers a multitude of benefits for your speaking voice. This chapter is loaded with valuable information for the speaker or businesswoman who wants to improve her voice skills or add singing to her presentations, as well as for the singer who wants to improve her technique.

Your Singing and Speaking Voices Have a Lot in Common

How did a television show about amateur singing hold onto the number one spot in the ratings year after year? Not even blockbuster movies or the biggest stars in Hollywood could knock it out of first place. The answer is simple. Next to winning the lottery, the biggest fantasy many people have is to stand in front of a cheering crowd, microphone in hand, singing their hearts out.

Realistically, not many of us have a chance to live out that dream on national television, but today it's easy to live that dream on a smaller scale. There really *is* a singer living inside of most of us, eagerly waiting for an opportunity to burst into song.

Music has always been part of the human experience and when it is expressed through a good singing, it can astound us. The authority of some singing voices can excite an entire stadium of people or calm a single distressed child. There is a special charisma that can only be found in the singing voice.

Singers Are Made, Not Born

I teach a class each month called "Anyone Can Sing," which is always attended by a diverse group of people—teachers, lawyers, counselors, salespeople, business executives, etc.—comprised mostly of women. Very seldom are they trained singers. The women range in age from 20 to 70. They come to the class with a passionate desire to sing, and a hope that someone will give them permission to do so. I love introducing women to their singing voices, especially those who are convinced that they don't have one.

The singing voice, just like the speaking voice, can carry with it a lot baggage. Singing is a very personal experience and all too many of us, growing up, are given reasons for why we can't or shouldn't sing. I had a choir teacher in fourth grade who always made me sit down when the group got up to sing because she said my voice was too loud. When I tell that story to my class, I always am amazed at how many people have someone like her in their lives and how her negative input silenced their voices—not only their singing voices but also their speaking voices as well—for years. Then again, it is the same voice. The only difference is, one is melodic and one is not.

Every exercise, every fact, and every example you'll find in this chapter applies to your singing voice as well as your speaking voice, including how you breathe, how you pronounce your words, and especially how you add power to your voice using the three dimensions of the voice: depth, width and length (see Chapter 3).

I often use singing to train a woman's speaking voice because when she is singing, her words and her breath are elongated, while the tone, or pitch of her voice, is moving up and down. Singing is like speaking in slow motion, with every word pulled and stretched like an elastic band. All of the physical working parts of your voice are also exaggerated while singing, from opening your mouth to extending your breath. In Chapter 6 we introduced you to your body's two diaphragms, the abdominal diaphragm, which pumps the air, and the pelvic diaphragm, which compresses the air. Obviously, it takes more breath control and vocal power to sing, than it does to speak. It also takes a very big mouth (acoustic hole) for your sound to come out. Have you ever noticed that strong singers have big mouths?

Anyone Can Sing

This section is for every woman who has said, "Singing is a gift that someone forgot to give to me." No matter how good a singer's natural talents are, most accomplished singers—amateur or professional—have had some form of vocal training. If they haven't, the minute they are signed by a label or a manager or become an *American Idol* finalist, they are introduced to the voice coach for a crash course in fine-tuning their vocal instrument. Consider your singing voice as a musical instrument just like a guitar or a trumpet. The big difference is you can't put your voice away in the closet when you're not using it. It goes where you go and shares your day, your problems, your distresses, and your *body*.

Learning how to use your body to sing properly is even more important than using your body to speak properly. That is because singing requires more physical power than speaking, and it takes a tremendous amount of energy to do it correctly.

Natural singing talent is rare and often based on the size of your vocal parts (nose, body, mouth) and your family's musical history (Nora Jones, Natalie Cole, Liza Minnelli all had a musical parent). Remember, as children we are great imitators of those around us, especially when it comes to our voices. If you grew up surrounded by talented singers, as many of today's second-generation singers have, good singing was simply a part of your upbringing. Still, even natural singers from musical family backgrounds recognize the value of good vocal training. Just as a pianist must learn how to play the piano correctly, a singer must learn how to sing correctly. If you are serious about your singing career, find a voice coach who resonates with you and your style of singing. If you are singing to improve your speaking voice and to gain more self-confidence, there are online voice lessons you can download for a reasonable fee. The bottom line is, we all have a voice—and with proper training can learn to use it correctly. When you play your vocal instrument correctly, good singing is a given.

Solving the Big "Who Done It!"

If used improperly, either your speaking or singing voice can suffer severe vocal damage. The question is—if you use both voices—how do you know which one is actually causing problems?

My early career was plagued with voice problems, including chronic hoarseness and often complete voice loss. I was singing seven nights a week in Las Vegas, and, like many of my professional clients, I just assumed my singing voice was doing the damage when, in fact, it was actually my speaking voice. Vocal loss is not always the fault of an overworked singing voice; it can just as easily be caused by tension in your speaking voice.

A few years ago, I worked with a very good singer whose chronic voice loss was jeopardizing her professional career. She was about to go into the studio to record her first CD and I was the third voice coach she had been to in six weeks. Her producer sent her to me as a last resort before voice surgery. I had worked with many singers with similar problems, and smugly told the producer," Sure, I can fix her."

We began working together and I found her singing technique, with a few minor adjustments, to be adequate. I also learned that she was working as a substitute teacher to supplement her income until she "hit the big time." Because I train both singers and speakers, I am always on red alert for signs of a person's vocal blowout. It turned out that her problem was the result of her speaking, not singing, technique.

Although the singing voice and the speaking voice use the same mechanism, they are located in different areas of the resonating system. The singing voice sits higher in the resonators (see Chapter 3 for a review), and when a singer knows how to use her voice correctly she can often sing, even when she can't talk.

After we had determined that my client's singing voice was fine, I set about training her speaking voice to sit higher in her resonating system and forward in her vocal cords. After a few sessions, the tension and weight she was putting on her voice while she was teaching began to lift, which automatically freed her singing voice. The moral is: Don't automatically assume that your singing voice is to blame for your vocal problems!

Singing for Your Health

Now that you know that you, too, can *learn* how to sing—and I have a stack of testimonials from women of all ages to prove it—

let's explore the health benefits that singing can bring to those who have the courage to pursue it.

Music, by itself, is a great healer and motivator—even without the addition of words. Each note on the musical scale has its own unique vibration and tone. When a note is played, it resonates (vibrates) at a certain rate of speed. Your body can physically feel the vibration and will resonate with each note. That is why some music *feels* good to us while other music doesn't. The volume at which music is played can also be a factor. Loud music pulses deeper into our bodies than soft music. Loud, energetic music is often played at political rallies and motivational seminars to influence the crowd into voting for a certain candidate or buying products at the back of the room—and it works. How many times have you bought books and CDs from a seminar, that you felt you *had* to have—but which in fact you've never touched?

- *The benefits of singing are not only good for your voice, but also can do wonders for your body, your mind, and your disposition.*

Music can be powerful, calming, energizing, and hypnotic. I have young students who come directly from school to their singing lessons. They come in with headaches, low energy, and stomach pains. The last thing they want to do is take a voice lesson, but after an hour of deep breathing, with music vibrating through their bodies, the joy of singing takes over, and the aches, the pains, and the stresses are gone. I have found this to be true for people of all ages. Singing is one of the best remedies for a stressed-out business life. That is why karaoke clubs are so prevalent in the Asian countries, where a good karaoke session after work is considered therapy. I absolutely agree; in fact, I believe that singing is not only good for the body, but also good for the overworked brain as well as for the soul. And it is fun.

Allergies, Asthma, and Your Voice

Allergies and asthma are two reasons women give for not singing. I can say from experience, not only do they *not* interfere with your singing, the mucus that allergies create in your sinus cavities actually enhances your resonance, creating a fuller sound in your voice. In addition, learning to breathe from the bottom of your lungs, not from the top, strengthens the air compressed by the pelvic diaphragm and shoots it up the bronchial tubes. This helps to clear congestion as it pushes the air up the windpipe, past the vocal cords, and out your nose and mouth. (Review Chapter 6 and practice the breathing exercises there.)

Voice problems such as a dry throat and scratchy vocal cords are often caused by the medication (decongestants and steroids) taken for allergies and asthma. Unfortunately, asthma and allergy sufferers can't stop taking their medications, but as the body's breathing mechanism gets stronger, most of my students find they don't need to take their medicine as often.

One of the major problems facing a singer or speaker with allergies is that as the sinuses fill, the voice has a strong nasal sound. It sounds as though you were pinching your nose saying, "I've got a cold in my nose" comes out like "Ib ga-da code ind by dose." Because the sound of your voice is all up in that high reso-nator where the Ms, Ns and INGs live, those three sounds end up doing extra duty contending with all of the mucus.

The trick when you speak or sing with allergies is to go light on any M, N, and ING, the opposite of what you learned about buzzing the Ms and Ns in Chapter 4. Instead of buzzing them, try pinching your nose as though it were stuffed up and say, "three blind mice." Now, with your nose still pinched, eliminate the N and the M, and say "three bli lice." No nasal sound, right? The trick is to tread lightly on the Ns, Ms, and INGs when you are singing or speaking with clogged sinuses. Look over the words to your song or speech and highlight all of the Ms, Ns, and INGs. Keep highlighting your lyrics until singing it that way becomes automatic. Just remember to go back to your normal resonant buzz when your nose is no longer stuffed. (This also helps when you have a plain old hateful head cold.)

Body Posture and Your Voice

"Watch your posture!" How many times did you hear that when you were growing up? For the singer or speaker, it's excellent advice because your posture has a direct effect on your vocal cords. Every actor, singer, and speaker needs to understand that there's a relationship between their body's balance point and their vocal performance, no matter the arena.

My studio walls are covered with full-length mirrors to help my students become aware of their posture, and the way they hold their head, neck, and upper body while singing and speaking. The tendency is to implode into the body, especially while singing the higher notes. Speakers also do this when they feel uncomfortable with their surroundings or their material. This tendency to collapse the head and neck puts extreme pressure and weight on your larynx and vocal cords, causing them to shut down. This action results in a tired, hoarse voice. In turn, as the head and neck collapse into the body, so go the shoulders and upper chest, causing restricted breathing. Because the voice is both an acoustic and a wind instrument, to work efficiently it needs big space and concentrated air. If we collapse our acoustic space by withdrawing into the neck and shoulders and drop our chest, which restricts the air supply to our lungs, we have placed our vocal mechanism in jeopardy simply because of bad posture.

This observation is not new; it was first made in the late 1800s by F. Matthias Alexander, a Shakespearean actor who suffered from chronic voice problems. He developed the Alexander Technique, which has been used effectively for over one hundred years by actors, singers, and business professionals to relax their voices and their bodies. It is like yoga for the vocal instrument. I have not experienced this technique personally, but have spoken with many people, especially women, who found it very helpful in relaxing the body before a performance. There are Alexander Technique facilitators all over the country and you can find many books and instructional CDs online.

If your neck, shoulders, and upper chest are tight and that is having an adverse effect on your voice, before you commit to any outside help, first get to know your own body posture. Start by installing a full-length mirror on the wall of the room where you practice singing or speaking. Watch yourself in the mirror while as you practice using your voice to make sure that your upper body is in alignment with your neck and shoulders. Next, make sure your jaw is in alignment with your neck (see Chapter 8). Awareness is the key to keeping all of your vocal parts in perfect balance and your posture erect. You might consider having someone video your next performance, presentation, or meeting so you can observe your movements and body posture in action. Being aware of your posture is the most effective way to correct poor posture.

Beating Dryness in the Voice

As I have often mentioned, your vocal cords need moisture to function properly. When singing or speaking with your mouth constantly open, and your breath coming in and out of it, the vocal cords can become very dry, which causes your voice to sound scratchy. Luckily, you can use a few simple techniques to help keep your cords moist.

1. *Inhale through your nose* as often as possible, especially when you are outside in cold weather. Your mouth is mostly open when you sing and speak, but when you have a break, it only takes a moment to moisturize you vocal cords with warm moist air coming through your nose.

2. *Sip water.* If possible, always have water handy on podium or bandstand, in the recording studio, and by your bed. A good technique for moisturizing your vocal cords is to take a sip of water and open your mouth to inhale while the mouth is still moisturized with water. Now take another sip and while the mouth is still awash with water, inhale again through the mouth. The inhalation of moist air will act as a humidifier as it is sucked down to the vocal cord area.

3. *Inhale steam.* Either use a humidifier or boil water on the stove, add a few drops of eucalyptus oil, cover your head with a towel, and inhale away. If you find yourself on the road in a hotel room, step into a hot shower and inhale that steaming moisture as far down your throat and into your lungs as you can get it.

4. *Bite your tongue.* This is my favorite remedy for a dry mouth and scratchy vocal cords: When you have no water handy and you mouth is dry, gently bite the tip of your tongue. Your salivary glands are triggered by the biting action because they think dinner is coming, causing the saliva to flow freely, which, in turn, moisturizes your mouth and drenches your vocal cords.

Body Language: Your Nonverbal Communicator

Sitting spellbound in the audience at a concert or a business seminar watching a skilled performer bring an entire audience to its feet applauding and cheering is a magical experience. To create this kind of excitement in a presentation or performance takes a mastery of technical skills, practice and preparation. It also takes the ability to communicate your songs or your message to your audience. To become an effective communicator requires a concentrated command of both your body and your voice: the body, for nonverbal communication, and the voice for verbal communication—spoken or sung. For the nonverbal part, you will use your body movements, facial expressions, hand gestures, and especially your eyes. Before you sing a note or speak a word, your audience is already reacting to these nonverbal communicators. This whole topic is fittingly called body language.

Your body can set a mood, express an opinion, and project an attitude to your audience simply by the way you move around the stage or platform or how you sit during a meeting or interview. When watching others, it's very helpful to take note of their body and facial movements. For example, do they close their eyes, look into the eyes of those to whom they are speaking or individuals in their audience, pace like a caged animal, appear uncomfortable standing behind the lectern or sitting in a chair, or do they "take the stage" as if they owned it?

Analyze what impresses or does not impress you about how they perform. You may notice some singers sing with their eyes closed, which can make the audience feel excluded, while some singers—and speakers—will look audience members directly in the eye, which can make some people feel very uncomfortable. Your facial expressions must draw your audience in, not shut them out or turn them off. This is true even if the audience is an audience of one.

Verbal communication, of course, emanates from your voice and the words you speak or sing. The exercises in Chapter 4, will help you add punch and expression to your singing and spoken words.

To move an audience with your words, you must first move yourself. No matter how many times I sing the same song or give the same class, I always approach it as if it is the first time. As I get excited, my audience gets excited with me. I have never been accused of being boring in my end-of-class evaluations, which I take as a compliment.

Adding Vitality to Your Presentation

If you are not filled with vitality and vivacity, your presentation or performance won't be either. Here are five things you can do to avoid making a low-key (read that "boring") presentation:

1. *Know your material inside and out.* Rehearse your songs or presentations until they become part of you. Don't try to fake your way through your performance; you will not fool any one but yourself.

2. *Determine the mood you want to create.* What do you wish your listener(s) to experience? Is it a love song, a political satire, dramatic reading, humorous keynote speech, or motivational speech? Each type of presentation or song carries a particular feeling with it, and your verbal and nonverbal communicators must be in sync with that feeling for your audience to be included.

3. *Draw on actual events* in your life that can trigger an emotion identical to the mood you want to create. Genuine emotion is hard to fabricate, and it takes a skilled actress to make it believable. I think of each three-minute song as the equivalent of a three-minute play, full of emotional ups and downs. A genuine performance can bring an

audience to tears, while an artificial performance can leave them cold. If you are a performer or a motivational speaker, a good acting class can come in handy. For the rest of us, practicing with friends and coworkers to project sincerity will suffice.

4. *Be energetic; energy is contagious.* During your presentation or performance, if your audience begins to shift in their seats, look at their watches, or talk to each other, it's time to give them an energy boost, break the mood, and bring the focus back to you. Remember, movement creates energy. If appropriate, play a game, have attendees stand, stretch, and rub each other's backs or have them pick a partner and go off to share a secret wish—techniques commonly used by motivational speakers. Even having them jog in place for a minute (you must do this too, of course) will bring more energy into the room. If you are running a meeting, suggest a coffee or restroom break, and so on. Be creative!

5. *Make them laugh.* People love to laugh; it makes them feel good and makes you appear approachable. If you are a singer, introduce your songs with *short*, humorous insights about the original singer, the song, or yourself. The emphasis here is on short. If you are a speaker or business executive, inside jokes about the company or coworkers are effective as long as they aren't negative or too personal—and you know the person you are talking about has a sense of humor.

Maximize Your Technique by Warming Up the Voice

Every athlete knows that the body must be pulled and stretched before an event. Those who skip the warm-up exercises run the risk of damaging their bodies. Singers, too, need to warm up before going on stage. While singing is more of an athletic event than speaking is, a wise speaker will take the time to gently plump up her vocal cords to avoid damaging them.

Because you need the entire body to create sound, simply warming up the voice is not enough. It takes a full body warm-up to relax the body and stretch the vocal muscles.

Voice Warm-Up Exercises

Sustained hum: Find a comfortable note in the middle of your range. With your lips closed, take a deep breath and hum the note for as long as you can. Time your hums and try to increase the amount of time until you can sustain the hum for 30 seconds or more.

Sirens: Do this exercise while standing upright. Fold a towel into a thick square and place it over your mouth to muffle the sound. Do ten sirens as loud as you can. Go from the top of your highest note down to your lowest note then back up again.

Do this for a few minutes, or until you feel your voice is flexible and able to hit the high notes with ease.

After you are finished with these two brief exercises, your voice will be ready to take on the world.

Ragdoll Warm-Up Exercise

With your feet flat on the floor, raise both arms over your head and stretch your fingers as high as you can reach. Bending at the waist, slowly drop your entire body over like a ragdoll hanging upside down. Your arms are limp and your head, neck, and shoulders are hanging down, completely relaxed. Begin to swing your arms side to side (like and elephant's trunk), allowing your head and neck to sway with them. While in this upside down position, with your mouth wide open, do ten yawn-sighs or sirens, starting with your highest down to your lowest note; you'll feel the sound coming out of your mouth without straining your vocal cords. Keeping your arms dangling, begin pulling yourself back up to a standing position one vertebra at a time. Allow your arms to reach over your head, stretching your fingers towards the ceiling. Repeat the entire ragdoll exercise two more times.

Relaxing the Head, Neck, and Shoulders Exercise

Roll your head slowly in a circle by dropping your chin on your chest—first to the right four times, then to the left four times. Let your arms hang down at your side. Drop your head down on your chest and lift it up and as far back as it will go, stretching your neck. Do these slowly ten times, then do ten shoulder rolls to the front and ten to the back. These exercises will loosen up the vocal cord area, the site of most of the tension when you speak or sing.

Limb Exercises

Arms and Hands: Shake your arms and hands as though you were shaking off water. Stretch with your arms at your sides then close your fingers in a fist slowly, ten times.

Leg Shakes: Stand on your right foot and vigorously shake your left foot and leg; then switch legs, and do the same thing with your right foot and leg. Keep alternating legs and shake each leg ten times.

Jaw Relaxing Exercise

Moving back to the head area, drop your jaw slowly then close it; make sure you do not shift it to the right or the left. Do this ten times, then place your fingers at the temporomandibular joint (see Chapter 8) on both sides and vigorously massage the area by moving your fingers in a circular direction for two minutes, until the joint feels loose and relaxed.

Breath Control Clock Warm-Up Exercise

With both feet slightly apart and your arms at your sides, move your right arm across your body to the left side and up past the head in a semicircle until your right hand is extended above your head and pointing in the 12 o'clock position. As the arm draws that semicircle, inhale slowly through your lips, as if you were sipping spaghetti.

With your lungs full of air, slowly move your hand and arm clockwise down towards 6 o'clock while slowly exhaling the air in a hiss. When your hand reaches 6 o'clock, inhale again and return your arm slowly to 12 o'clock. Repeat this exercise five times.

How to Use a Microphone

Everyone who speaks or sings at some time will be handed a microphone. Some people come alive with a "mike" in their hands; others completely freeze. Basic microphone technique involves knowing the distance between the microphone and your mouth and where to aim it.

Let's start with aim. Most vocal mikes are designed to pick up the voice, not the surrounding sounds of the band or audience. The focal point of a vocal mike is about the size of a dime—if your voice is not hitting that spot, it will get lost. If your audience can't hear you, no matter how important or your material, they soon lose interest. If you are what professional sound people call a "mike-eater"—someone who plants his or her lips on the mike and yells—the voice becomes muffled, garbled, and extremely irritating to the audience. An uncomfortable audience is not a receptive audience. Even the best performance, song, or presentation can be ruined by a bad sound system or poor mike technique.

The second factor is distance. As a rule of thumb, a handheld mike should be about one inch from your mouth. If it drifts to the left or right, your audience won't hear your words or the notes you sing. I tell my students to think of a microphone as their favorite ice cream cone and keep it within licking distance.

Here is a good tip to help you stay within your microphone's working distance. Visualize your mike as your best friend's ear. You would never yell full volume in her ear, nor would you stand five feet away to tell her about last night's date. You also wouldn't turn your head away and expect her to hear what you are saying.

Some instructors advise that you "eat" the mike, and some advise that you pull it away on the loud, high notes. There are many factors involved in determining how much of your voice is enough for your audience. If *you* can't hear your voice, the tendency is to keep upping your volume until you can hear it. That doesn't work, because unless you are wearing ear monitors or standing in front of a stage monitor, the chances of you hearing your own voice are slim. Your best volume gauge is the *feel* of your voice, not the *sound* of it. If it feels strained while singing or speaking, there is a good chance your voice is coming over the speakers strained and too loud.

There are four types of microphones used today by "live" performers:

1. *Basic hand-held microphone* with a short or long cord attached. This is an old-fashioned system that limits the speaker's movement to the length of their cord. If part of your presentation involves going out into your audience and your cord is too short, it can restrict your performance.

2. *Cordless microphone* that runs on batteries. This type of mike is bulky but has no cord limitation. If you are fortu-

nate enough to have a sound engineer running your system, that person will be responsible for keeping your mike running. If you are using a "house system," make sure that your mike has a fresh battery in it. If your battery runs out in the middle of your song or your talk, changing batteries can break the momentum of your performance. (It has happened to me more than once, even with a professional engineer running the equipment, so I carry an extra 9-volt battery in my equipment bag.)

Although there is no cord limitation with a cordless mike, there can be transmission issues relating to distance and frequencies that may restrict your movements. Much like your cell phone, there can be dead areas in the room or hall in which you are performing. Singers and speakers who use their mikes as props often prefer hand-held mikes. They feel much more comfortable holding their mike with one hand and using the other to gesture, than having to figure out what to do with *two* hands.

Always check before your performance to see what types of microphones are available to you.

3. *Lavaliere or lapel microphone.* This type is used mainly by speakers and seminar leaders who need two hands to hold up materials, work their PowerPoint presentations, and record their workshops. It takes a professional sound engineer with a soundboard to monitor this type of microphone. It is crucial to your performance that you know *before* you perform what kind of sound system is available to you. When it comes to your sound, you do not want any surprises. The quality of a sound system can make or break your performance.

4. *Cordless headset.* Anyone who wears an older cordless headset with the microphone in front of her mouth automatically looks like a rock star (a la Madonna). The newer versions, however, are very high tech, offer quality sound

for both singers and speakers, and are almost invisible to the audience. They allow total movement of both hands and body and are perfect for the confident singer/speaker who knows what to do with her hands. Headset microphones also require a professional sound engineer.

How to Have Fun and Gain Experience at the Same Time

Women often tell me, "I'd love to sing, but I don't know where to go to sing." I always say, "When you *learn* how to sing well, there will be plenty of places to sing!" and there always are. This is also true for speakers.

I'm constantly amazed at what pops up when a singer or speaker feels confident, not only with her ability, but also with herself. There are weddings, talent shows, church solos, worship groups, and rehearsal bands looking for singers; your can try out for community theater shows, sing the National Anthem at Little League or school ball games, and do volunteer work with children or with seniors at retirement facilities. For speakers, there are meetings, workshops, online educational websites looking for things to add to their databases. Don't waste your time wondering where you will sing or speak; spend that time learning your craft and the world will find you—it always does.

Your Voice in Review

After each of my classes but before I send everyone home to practice what they have learned, I always spend time answering their questions. Over the years, I've learned that as long as someone has questions about their voice and its mechanics, they will be hesitant about doing what is required to improve their voices. Old habits do die hard and many women's voice problems are the result of bad habits. As you might imagine, I love the human female voice. Its capacity for variety is endless while its restrictions are only those that we unwittingly put on it.

It's been rumored that the average person needs to hear new information seven times before it sinks in. Since this is a "smart" woman's guide to a powerful and persuasive voice, I believe that a quick review of some of the key points in this book will suffice.

Keeping Your Voice Healthy

At some time in a person's career, every singer, speaker, and business professional will come face to face with a vocal problem. There's no need to panic. These eight tips will save the day and keep your voice going strong even when you're not feeling one hundred percent.

Tip #1: Don't take decongestants if you have to use your voice. A decongestant's job is to dry up the mucus in your body. Your vocal cords are mucous membranes and thrive on that mucus. If you dry it up, your voice will sound and feel rough and scratchy.

Tip #2: Just resting your voice will not *solve your vocal problems.* Many vocal problems result from the overuse and abuse of your vocal cords. Resting is helpful, but if you do not learn how to use your voice correctly, the symptoms will return. Good voice technique is always your best answer.

Tip #3: Never whisper if you are losing your voice. Whispering will further damage your vocal cords. Try not to speak. Write notes if necessary.

Tip #4: Never use cough drops containing menthol if you are going to speak or sing. Menthol freezes and shrinks your vocal cords. To work efficiently, they must be warm and plumped, not cold and shrunken. Good old-fashioned lemon drops will do the trick, and the sour effect will create saliva—your vocal cords natural lubricant.

Tip #5: Don't clear your throat strenuously. Excessive throat clearing is a very harmful habit. The more you try to clear out the mucus, the more mucus will be created to protect your vocal cords. It is a never-ending battle that you cannot win. Instead, open your mouth in a big yawn and say Haaaaaaaaaa. Use the air as a Roto-Rooter to gently clear the debris on your vocal cords.

Tip #6: Become the master of your jaw. This is vital to good voice projection and vocal longevity. With good vocal technique and a healthy body, your voice only improves with age. Isn't that good news? Keep your voice relaxed by relaxing your jaw.

Tip #7: Strengthen your abdominal diaphragm's pumping action. The vocal cords work like valves and need a strong supply of compressed air to perform their magic. Stick your tongue out and do the "pant like a dog" exercise to strengthen your pumping action.

Tip #8: Both heated air and air conditioning dehydrate your vocal cords. For the sake of your voice, turn them both off while you sleep. If you live in a cold climate and must use the heating system, be sure to use a humidifier by your bed.

Twenty Facts to Remember about Your Voice

Good voice training should be part of every woman's basic business training. A smart woman will learn proper vocal technique *before* the big opportunities come. After all, you want to be ready for that interview with Oprah or the chance to sing at your best friend's wedding. Preparation is the key to unlocking your limitless supply of self-confidence, and self-confidence is required to unlock the doors to professional and personal success.

Drill these 20 basic facts deeply into your brain until they become a permanent part of your belief system. Your vocal parts have no brain of their own, and only believe what you believe. That's *Fact #1.*

Fact #2: A powerful voice must be able to go in three directions at the same time: down for depth and power, first dimension; wide for fullness and emotion, second dimension; and out of the mouth for length and control, third dimension. (To practice your 3-Dimensional Voice, do the exercises in Chapter 3.)

Fact #3: No quick vocal fix is ever a substitute for good voice technique.

Fact #4: With good vocal technique and a healthy body, your voice only improves with age. Give yourself a daily voice lift (see Chapter 8).

Fact #5: Nodules on the vocal cords (calluses) are caused by one thing and one thing only, poor vocal technique. Surgery cannot cure poor technique.

Fact #6: Smoking is the worst thing you can do to your voice.

Fact #7: Verbal abuse can cause severe vocal stress and damage to the vocal cords. Keep your relationships stress-free for the sake of your voice (and your mental health)—and the rest of your body.

Fact #8: A weak voice is a symptom. To strengthen your voice, you must find the cause.

Fact #9: Throughout a woman's life, her hormones will have a major effect on her voice. A good understanding of that fact will eliminate years of frustration.

Fact #10: A good voice is within every woman's grasp if she takes the time to learn how to use her voice correctly.

Fact #11: Every woman has five voices to sing with, not just one.

Fact #12: Power breathing adds control and strength to a weak voice.

Fact #13: Stage fright is simply your body's reaction to anxiety.

Fact #14: You have two diaphragms, one to pump and one to compress the air you breathe.

Fact #15: The vocal cords work like valves and need a strong supply of compressed air to perform their magic. Keep pumping that air.

Fact #16: No matter what size your mouth is, to be heard all the way to the back of the room it must be *open*.

Fact #17: If your voice is your livelihood, and you work in a tense, negative environment, the minute you feel your voice reacting by raising the pitch and gripping the throat area, take a moment to yawn-sign it back to a relaxed position. Your voice can not correct itself in that raised larynx position.

Fact #18: Men do not hear vocal tones in the same way women hear them. High-pitched sounds are actually painful to many male ears. Remember, it's not personal, so to be most effective in your communication, modulate the pitch of your voice when speaking to a man.

Fact #19: One voice does not fit all situations. Learn to play with all 36 voices listed in Chapter 2. Vocal variety *is* the spice of life.

Fact #20: Whether speaking or singing, you and you alone are the master of your vocal instrument. Take the time to learn how to play it correctly and your voice will be a delight to all of the ears it reaches, and a bonus to your success.

In Conclusion

By reading this book and doing the exercises in it, I hope you have come to a new understanding and respect for your unique and amazing voice. I love interactive communication—my e-mail is happily open to your questions. I am also a work in progress and many of your questions open doors to new areas of interest and discovery about the many aspects of the female voice. As your experiences with your voice are added to my information base, I can in turn share them with women all over the world who need to find their own voices.

Margaret Mead, one of the most influential female thinkers of all time, said, "Never doubt that a small group of thoughtful committed people can change the world. Indeed, it's the only thing that ever has." As each woman finds her own voice, that small group grows in intensity and the voices get louder until someone hears the message and takes action. Remember, it's not always our words that people hear, it's how we say our words that gets the attention. As Maya Angelou said so brilliantly, "Words mean more than what is set down on paper. It takes the human voice to infuse them with shades of deeper meaning." Please let that voice be yours.

Appendix

References, Recommended Study

Alburger, James. *The Art of Voice Acting.* Boston: Focal Press, 2002.

Blumenfield, Robert. *Accents.* New York: Limelight Editions, 2000.

Carlson, Richard. *Don't Sweat the Small Stuff.* New York: Barnes and Nobel Publishing, 2007.

Cooper, Morton. *Change Your Voice, Change Your Life.* New York: HarperCollins Publishing, 1998.

Gardenswartz, Lee, Ph.D., and Anita Rowe, Ph.D. *What It Takes.* New York: Doubleday, 1987.

Goodman, Ted, (editor). *Forbes Book of Business Quotations.* New York: Black Dog & Leventhal Publishers, 1997.

Jacobi, Jeffery. *How to Say It with Your Voice.* Englewood Cliffs, N.J.: Prentice-Hall Press, 1996.

Montoya, Peter. *The Brand Called You.* Tustin, Calif.: Personal Branding Press, 2005.

Leech, Thomas. *How to Prepare, Stage, and Deliver Winning Presentations.* New York: AMACOM, 1993.

Orman, Suze. *Women & Money: Owning the Power to Control Your Destiny.* New York: Random House, 2007.

Pestrak, Debra. *Playing with the Big Boys.* Carlsbad Calif.: Sun Publications, 2001.

Penskey, Raleigh. *101 Ways to Promote Yourself.* New York: Avon Books, 1997.

Richardson, Cheryl. *Take Time for Your Life.* New York: Broadway Books, 1998.

Roberts, Cokie. *Ladies of Liberty.* New York: HarperCollins, 2008.

Thomas, Marlo. *The Right Words at the Right Time.* New York: Atria Books, 2002.

Tracy, Brian. *Speak to Win*. New York: AMACOM, 2008.

Sataloff, Robert, M.D. *Professional Voice*. New York: Raven Press, 1991.

Walters, Lilly. *What to Say When You're Dying on the Platform*. New York: McGraw-Hill, Inc., 1995.

Additional Training Resources

Online Voice Classes: virtualvoicecoach.com

Karaoke Tracks and CDs: pocketsong.com

Toastmasters International: www.toastmasters.com

For additional voice information, tips, resources, and to chat with Joni visit: thevoiceofsuccessblog.com

Women's Organizations

American Bar Association
750 N Lakeshore Drive
Chicago IL 60611
Phone: (312) 988-5497
According to the ABA, 29.1 percent of American lawyers are women, with *more than 308,000 female attorneys in the U.S.*

American Women in Radio And Television
1101 Connecticut Avenue NW, Suite 100
Washington DC 20036
Phone: (202) 429-5102
FAX: (202) 223-4579
2,400 members. 50 chapters and/or state affiliates.

National Association for Female Executives
127 West 24th Street
New York NY 10011
or
c/o J. Symons
927 15th Street NW
Washington DC 20005
Phone: (202) 289-8538
250,000 members. 400 local networks.

Business And Professional Women/USA
1620 Eye Street NW, Suite 210
Washington DC 20006
BPW has a national network of over 100,000 members.

Women in Communications, Inc.
2101 Wilson Blvd, Suite 417
Arlington VA 22201
Phone: (703) 528-4200
Fax: (703) 528-4205
Women in Communications, Inc., one of the nation's oldest and largest
    communications organizations, has more than 12,000 members ac-
    tive in print and broadcast journalism, public relations, marketing,
    business and association communications, advertising, magazine and
    book publishing, communications education and law, photojournal-
    ism, film, and design.
12,000+ members. 83 professional chapters; 104 student chapters.

American Association of University Women (AAUW)
1111 16th Street NW
Washington DC 20036
Phone: (202) 785-7700
Fax: (202) 872-1425
AAUW is a national organization of 135,000 college graduates focusing
    on advocacy for equity and education for women.
135,000 members. 1,800 chapter and/or state affiliates.

Teachers

National Association for Women in Education
Phone: (202) 659-9330
According to NEA (National Education Association) research, *75percent
    of the nation's 3 million teachers are women!*

Speakers Groups

Toastmasters International

Charters its *10,000 clubs and has more than 200,000 members in 90 countries*. For information, visit *www.toastmasters.org*.

National Speakers Association

Meeting Professional International has *17,200 members.* For Information, visit www.nsaspeaker.org.

Index

diphthongs, 79–80
Don't Sweat the Small Stuff (Richard Carlson), 97
double vowels, 79–80
dropped larynx position, 55
dry throat, 17, 155, 159–160, 191–192

ear monitors, 199
effective female business voice, 25
elongating a sound, 71, 78, 81
emotional stress, 57
 and PMS, 151
 and TMJ, 18
emotional temperature gauge, 130, 137
emotions, 5–6
 in love relationships, 137
 as part of vital energy, 90
 in presentations, 194–195
 uncontrolled, 137
 and your vocal personality, 121–129
 and your voiceprint, 130
energetic delivery, 173–176, 195
entertaining presentations, 173
explosive consonants, 75, 77
eye contact, 45

facial expressions, 29, 70
facts about your voice, 6–7, 203–206
failure, 169
fast talkers, 81, 133
fear(s)
 facing, 98–99
 of public speaking, 10, *see also* stage fright
 of voice loss, 7

female voice, *see* women's voices
fight or flight response, 86, 87
Filler Awareness Exercise, 85
filler words, 84, 85
Finding That "G" Spot Exercise, 68–69
Find Your Voice Exercise, 69–71
first impressions, 135, 137
flop sweat, 173
flu, 139–142
freeing your voice, 18–19
fricative consonants, 75–76
full voice, loud voice vs., 48, 107–108

gender differences in voices, 4, 10–12
gestures, 178
girth factor, 107
glides, 76
glottal fry, 124
grace-days clause, 151

hand-held microphone, 199
hands, what to do with, 178
happiness, 38
harsh-raspy voice, 122
hating your voice, 14–15
headaches, 58
head resonator, 50
health
 of the body, 59
 of the voice, 202–203, *see also* problem(s) affecting the voice
hearing your own voice, 13–14, 48–49, 199
heartburn, 143–144
heated air, 203

About the Author

Joni Wilson is an internationally recognized voice expert, professional speaker, and bestselling author with over 18 years experience training both the speaking and the singing voice. She has taught master classes for the Learning Annex in San Diego and Hollywood, and has been a featured keynote speaker and seminar leader for women's conferences and business workshops. Her clients include business executives with major corporations, professional speakers, singers, actors, and even an *American Idol* finalist. Her speaking voice classes for the National Speakers Association have gained her recognition and praise from her fellow speakers, and her online voice lessons at virtualvoicecoach .com have generated thank yous and bravos from grateful clients worldwide.

Joni is the creator of the 3-Dimensional Voice® Training System, the cutting-edge voice method so effective it is changing the lives of speakers, entertainers and business professionals all over the world. As a professional singer and entertainer, Joni has hosted a TV talk show, performed stand-up comedy, was an opening act for Elvis (the real one), and owned and operated a dinner theater in Colorado. Her joy is singing with a swinging big band when she is not speaking, teaching, or writing.

Joni, who is included in the *Yearbook of Experts*, is the veteran of over 50 radio interviews and is a frequent guest on television talk shows including Fox News. She brings the expertise of a master voice trainer, who has "been there and done it all" to her workshops, and teaches with the wit and humor of a seasoned entertainer. She is passionate about sharing her vast knowledge of the female voice with women who are ready to "step up" and let their voices be heard.